BUILDING CHAMPIONS

Success Principles from A-to-Z

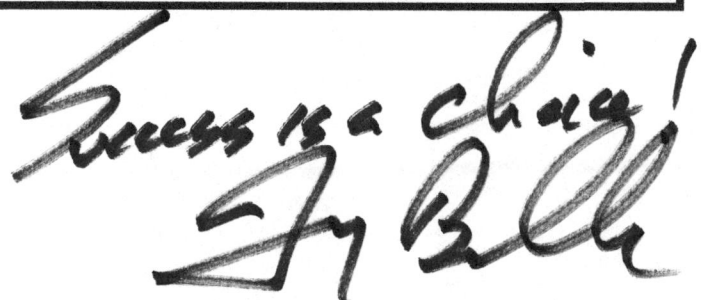

JAMY BECHLER
Author of *The Leadership Playbook*

Copyright © 2018 by Jamy Bechler
www.JamyBechler.com

All rights reserved. No part of this publication may be reproduced, stored in a retrieval system, or transmitted, in any form or by any means, electronic, mechanical, photocopying, recording, or otherwise, without the prior written permission of the author, except in the case of brief quotations embodied in critical reviews and certain other noncommercial uses permitted by copyright law.

For permission requests, write to the author, with the subject "Permission Request," at the email address Support@CoachBechler.com.

Because of the dynamic nature of the Internet, any web addresses contained in this book may have changed since publication and may no longer be valid.

ISBN: 0-9992125-2-4
ISBN-13: 978-0-9992125-2-3

Quantity or Team Sales are available by contacting BuildingChampions@JamyBechler.com

Cover Designed by Mathoni Villegas.

Special Thanks to Tristen Gonzalez and Megan Welch for their research and editing efforts. Without them, this book wouldn't have been possible.

This book is dedicated to my parents – Frank and Beth – who instilled in me the very characteristics that are contained in this book. They are true role models and champions, helping to shape me so that I could then pay it forward and positively influence others. Thanks, mom and dad!

CONTENTS

Success Is A Choice 1
Attitude 4
Belief 8
Courage 12
Determined 15
Effort 19
Fundamentals 22
Grit 26
Honorable 30
Ideals 35
Journey 38
Knowledge 43
Listening 47
Mental Toughness 51
Next Play 55
Open-Minded 60
Preparation 64
Quality 70
Resiliency 75
Strength 79
Trust 84
Unselfish 89
Valuable 93
Work Ethic 97
X-Factor 100
Yes 105
Zest 110
Final Thoughts 114
Notes 119
Excerpt from *The Leadership Playbook* 127

SUCCESS IS A CHOICE

"Champions do not become champions when they win an event, but in the hours, weeks, months, and years they spend preparing for it."
~ Michael Jordan

"Success isn't owned. It's leased, and rent is due every day."
~ J.J. Watt

"Champions are made from something they have deep inside them; a desire, a dream, a vision."
~ Muhammad Ali

"Negative thoughts are the nails that build a prison of failure. Positive thoughts will build you a masterpiece."
~ Jon Gordan

"I do not judge success based on championships; rather, I judge it on how close we came to realizing our potential."
~ John Wooden

Alan Stein, Jr. is considered one of the top performance coaches in the nation. For years he has worked with some of the best basketball players in the world. In fact, when I was a basketball coach, I used many of his conditioning drills for my teams. I even interviewed him on my "Success is a Choice" podcast and you can listen to this episode by visiting www.JamyBechler.com/AlanStein.

Alan once told me about his first encounter with Kobe Bryant back in 2007 when he was in his prime and considered the best player in the world. Nike flew Alan out to the Kobe Bryant Skills Camp. He was so intrigued by all of the talk of how insane Kobe's individual workouts were and wanted to see for himself.

He asked Kobe if he could watch one of these famous workouts and the Lakers guard told him he'd be starting his workout at 4:00 a.m. Alan, who set his alarm for 3:00 a.m., wanted to beat Kobe to the gym but was unsuccessful. Kobe was already dripping with sweat with a warm up before his workout was in full swing by the time Alan arrived.

Alan recalled how he was bored to death because for the first 45 minutes, Kobe was practicing basics that any middle schooler would do. Later that day Alan asked Kobe why the best player in the world was spending so much time on the basics. Kobe replied, **"Why do you think I'm the best player in the world? Because I never ever get bored with the basics."**

You see, even though he was focusing on the basics, he was attacking those basics with an unmatched attention to detail and ferocious competitiveness. He didn't just practice until he got it right. He was practicing until he couldn't do it wrong.

Chuck Noll, the Hall of Fame Pittsburgh Steelers head coach once said, **"Champions are champions not because they do anything extraordinary but because they do ordinary things better than anybody else."**

This book is about basic building blocks and fundamentals necessary for achieving success and maximizing potential. The 26 traits presented in this book are not the only ones that can help lead to success, but they are important. The more that you can master the fundamentals, the better your chances to maximize your potential. We should always be focused on becoming the best version of ourselves.

UCLA basketball coach John Wooden won 10 NCAA Championships in a span of 12 years. Despite this astounding achievement, he measured success in a different way. He always said, **"Success is peace of mind which is a direct result of self-satisfaction in knowing you did your best to become the best you are capable of becoming."**

Kareem Abdul-Jabbar wrote a book in 2017 entitled *Coach Wooden and Me: Our 50 Year Friendship On and Off the Court.* Coach Wooden valued his relationship with Kareem more than the 3 titles he won when Kareem played center for him at UCLA. Here's the great thing about becoming better as a person – those same traits can also directly lead to success in sports, business, or the community.

Yes, we want to be winners on the scoreboard, but winning in life will ultimately be more important and can lead to a life of significance. Success is a choice. What choice will we make today?

ATTITUDE

"Most folks are about as happy as they make up their minds to be."
~ Abe Lincoln

"A bad attitude is like a flat tire. You can't go anywhere until you change it."
~ Unknown

"Life is 10% what happens to you and 90% how you react to it."
~ Charles Swindoll

"Don't count the days, make the days count."
~ Muhammad Ali

"A positive attitude gives you power over your circumstances instead of your circumstances having power over you."
~ Dr. Joyce Meyer

The great British Statesman Winston Churchill once said, "For myself I am an optimist - it does not seem to be much use being anything else". Positivity is so often disregarded by realists as naïve or unrealistic, but Sir Winston Churchill wasn't an ignorant man or someone to who lived with his head in the clouds. He was a well-respected man who inspired others to greatness.

He knew that the only way to overcome overwhelming odds was to have a positive can-do attitude. Being positive doesn't mean that we ignore the negative or the challenges that we face, but rather that we overcome the negative through a positive mindset and finding solutions.

Our team may be playing a team that is ranked much higher and we have to maintain a positive attitude. Maybe our team is down a few points, goals, or baskets and it seems impossible to recover the deficit. The truth is that sometimes underdog teams win the game and sometimes a big come back happens, but this only happens if a team and players maintain a positive attitude and are fearless enough to keep believing that the unlikely can happen.

In the sports world, a game or championship may be at stake. For Winston Churchill, an entire nation's freedom was at stake. Despite all odds, England and the Allies defeated Nazi Germany in World War II.

One of Winston Churchill's most famous quotes is when he said, "The pessimist sees the difficulty in every opportunity. The optimist sees the opportunity in every difficulty." A positive attitude is so crucial, because it affects how one views a situation. How we view a situation affects our course of action and the enthusiasm and momentum that we can generate from it.

Positive people do not allow circumstances to dictate how they feel. They do not get discouraged easily. They make sure that their attitude dictates how they look at a situation. When we refuse to be victims of the circumstances, then we may actually take actions that can influence the situation. We may have now missed the opportunity at hand. Once we feel like we have the power to change the situation we are motivated to take action and be proactive

Attitude

towards achieving our goals.

As the seemingly unbeatable Nazi's conquered much of Europe during World War 2, it seemed to most people as if Germany and Hitler would ultimately reach Great Britain, as well. But Churchill had other ideas. He knew that the situation might keep getting direr but that they could ultimately win – even when many of his advisors expected him to call for retreat or surrender.

On June 4, 1940 (before the United States entered the war), Churchill gave a speech to the House of Commons of the Parliament of the United Kingdom. In this speech he said, "We shall defend our island, whatever the cost may be, we shall fight on the beaches, we shall fight on the landing grounds, we shall fight in the fields and in the streets, we shall fight in the hills; we shall never surrender." [1]

One man's positive attitude and relentless belief brought hope to a nation; a hope to press on in the fight and a hope to believe that victory could be attained.

The power of a positive attitude is not shown amidst great achievement, but instead great failure. It is easy to define success as a championship, a personal record, or obtaining recognition; these things quickly fade, and old trophies rust in a cabinet. True success is having a positive attitude when things do not go as planned again and again and again. Success will come to one who does not give into discouragement and give up.

An attitude defines how a person, team, or leader of a nation will respond to adversity. A positive attitude defines if they will succeed. Churchill did not allow Great Britain to fall to the Nazis because his attitude was contagious. He led the nation through courage and positivity.

Legendary USA Basketball and Duke University head coach Mike Krzyzewski says, "Don't worry about losing, think about winning." We will face challenges and adversity but if we have a positive attitude – if we choose to be a winner – then we'll see these challenges as building blocks, stepping stones, and opportunities.

Remember, thinking positive and having a good attitude doesn't mean that we'll never face challenges. That is wishful thinking, not positive thinking. Having a positive attitude means that you'll have the proper mindset to find solutions and not be fixated on problems. Every day, we'll be faced with choices. We can choose to be positive and move forward or we can dwell on the negative and remain stuck in the mud. Negative thinkers see the difficulty in every opportunity, but a positive thinker sees an opportunity in every difficulty.

BELIEF

"He who says he can and he who says he can't are both usually right."
~ Confucius

"If you don't have confidence, you'll always find a way not to win."
~ Carl Lewis

"A bird sitting on a tree is never afraid of the branch breaking, because her trust is not on the branch but on her own wings. Believe in yourself."
~ Unknown

"If you believe it will work out, you'll see opportunities. If you believe it won't, you will see obstacles."
~ Wayne Dyer

"You have to believe in yourself when no one else does."
~ Serena Williams

From 2011-2014, the Houston "Lastros" (as many mockingly called the Astros) averaged 104 losses per year out of the 162 games they would play each year. They were a laughingstock among Major League Baseball fans. Not only were they the worse team but they also had the lowest payroll, so they weren't seen as much of a threat anytime soon. Their stadium was eerily empty most games and those that did attend seemed to enjoy booing more than cheering their hometown team.

After a few years of struggle, those "Lastros"

whom no one believed in started to gel. They started to believe in themselves. They started to develop. They started to win – and win big! They made *Sports Illustrated* look smart as they fulfilled the magazine's 2014 cover predicted that they would be the 2017 World Series Champions. From worst to first in only three short years. One of the greatest underdog stories. How did they do it?

It was a team of executives alongside many players and coaches all believing that their time to shine and their opportunity would one day come. They believed they needed a growing period, they needed to create a different atmosphere, and then they could create a highly competitive program. They were completely reorganizing the roster and the way the program ran, in essence, starting over.

They weren't an organization that believed they were perfect or believed they were incapable of making mistakes but rather, Sports Illustrated said, "their goal was to make marginally more correct decisions than their competitors". They just believed in giving their best effort. [1]

When things go wrong for us as competitors, it's easy for us to believe what everyone else says. It is easy to turn our backs on everything we know and instantly doubt. It is easy to believe people who have no idea what we have gone through to get where we are today. We must continue to believe, because of everything that we have invested in our game and our success. We are investing in ourself. We must believe in ourself.

It's easy to encounter a setback and immediately turn on your teammates or coaches, but

Belief

successful players keep believing. When times get tough, that's when the true leaders come out and that's when quitters do what they do best – quit. Adversity reveals what we truly believe about ourselves and those around us. It's a true test of our character. Never stop believing in what we are capable of.

Tom Brady is also a great example of belief. Brady was on the football team at the University of Michigan where he sat on the bench for two years and didn't play until his junior year. He was a solid college player but was not a top prospect as evidenced by the fact he was drafted in the NFL in the sixth round as the 199th pick. He only played in one game his first season for the New England Patriots. He was originally the fourth string quarterback and then a few unfortunate events led him to be the backup.

With an unfortunate injury to the starting quarterback in only the second game of the season, Brady got his chance to shine, took advantage of it and never looked back as he became arguably the greatest quarterback in NFL history.

Brady, just like the Astros, believed in what he was capable of. He knew that it did not matter what anyone else said and he knew that their doubt and skepticism was irrelevant. He believed that his chance would come, and boy, did it. Imagine if he would have quit or transferred when he was sitting at the University of Michigan?

Underdog stories are created, most often, by people believing in the impossible or improbable. The so-called underdogs are just people believing that they can accomplish more than what others think. They make themselves unstoppable. They create their own luck. There is a long-time quote that says, "Luck is just when preparation meets opportunity." We can't get lucky if you don't believe that we can. Underdogs are so hungry for success that they keep working hard to make sure it happens.

Success isn't built in a day. It takes time and it takes belief. Champions believe in themselves. It does not matter what their circumstances are and it does not matter what others have to say. Champions continue to believe in themselves, even when no one else does.

COURAGE

"All our dreams can come true, if we have the courage to pursue them."
~ Walt Disney

"Courage is not just walking into the lion's den but also locking the gate behind you."
~ Michael Sage

"Courage is being scared to death and saddling up anyway."
~ John Wayne

"A Ship is safe in harbor, but that's not what ships are for."
~ William G.T. Shedd

"Courage is fear holding on a minute longer."
~ General George S. Patton

Courage is something that everyone hopes they have. Many people say that they are brave until a true test comes and then they find out for sure. Most of us struggle with being brave or courageous. It is easy to hesitate, freeze, or let doubt creep in at the moment of truth.

On January 15, 2009, Captain Chelsey "Sully" Sullenberger had the opportunity to put his courage (and training) to the test. He was the pilot of US Airways Flight 1549 when it hit a flock of geese shortly after takeoff from New York's LaGuardia Airport. Both engines were damaged. Captain Sullenberger had to decide in an instant what the best thing to do, not only for him, but for his 155 passengers. All of his experience as a fighter pilot for the United States Air Force, as well as his time as a commercial airline pilot, would come down to this moment.

A lot of times we seem to forget about all the preparation it takes to become successful, or we lose track of what we are really working towards. We don't take pride or put enough importance on the little things.

Unfortunately, we can't just wake up one day and instantaneously be successful. It comes with time. It comes with preparation. It comes with believing that the process we're embarking on will lead us to our destination. It comes with doing the little things every day. Courage is knowing that we are doing the right thing no matter the circumstances, and in a matter of seconds, Captain Sully demonstrated just that.

Once Sully called in for an emergency, air traffic operators advised him with several landing sites as options. However, he made the decision that landing on the Hudson River was the best place to ensure the safety of everyone aboard due to the lack of time. Captain Sully was fully prepared and able to make this courageous decision for the sake of all the passengers aboard Flight 1549. With more than 35 years of experience, he was confident enough to execute on the courage that would be needed to do something so extreme as landing in the water.

He landed the plane in the Hudson River, swam through the water-filled plane making sure that all passengers were okay, and made sure he was the last

Courage

person to evacuate. Amazingly, all 155 people were able to escape serious injury.

In a moment, he was thrust into making a decision that could cost so many people their lives. Captain Sully was able to be courageous because of his preparation. He knew that he had the ability to land the plane in the Hudson because of his years of preparation for a scary moment like this. Of course, the moment was scary, but he was able to overcome that fear. He even went so far as to make sure everyone was evacuated from the plane before evacuating himself. He was courageous in risking his life for the sake of others.

Preparation and practice make the big games not so big. Once we start to experience success, we cannot forget what got us there. Once we get to those big, important matches, it's time to be courageous and step up knowing that we are equipped to do this again. Be brave and ready to face anything that stands in the way of you and success.

If we prepare, if we work day in and day out, believing in the process, and always doing the little things when it is time, we will be able to be stronger than fear, anxiety, or lack of preparation. We will rise and be courageous. We will know we have nothing to fear.

DETERMINED

"The difference between the impossible and the possible lies in a person's determination."
~ Tommy Lasorda

"I believe that success is achieved by ordinary people with extraordinary determination."
~ Zig Ziglar

"If you set goals and go after them with all the determination you can muster, your gifts will take you places that will amaze you."
~ Les Brown

"When the will is ready the feet are light."
~ Ancient Proverb

"There are no secrets to success. It is the result of preparation, hard work, and learning from failure."
~ Colin Powell

How many "NO's" does it take for us to stop believing in ourselves? When people tell us we can't, how fast do we give up on ourselves? Do we listen to the haters? Even worse, do we believe the haters?

Walt Disney was a man who believed in himself and his dreams. Think of how popular he is today and how much success the Walt Disney Company has achieved. It wasn't always Mickey ears and Disney princesses for Walt. While working at a newspaper, the young cartoonist was told he lacked creativity. Imagine that. Walt Disney, the creator of all things childlike, magical, and fantastic was told

Determined

he didn't have the right stuff. He would then go on to form Laugh-O-Gram Films ... which eventually failed. He was still determined. Though he was essentially broke, Walt decided that he would use the last of his money to go to Hollywood determined to make his dreams come true.

He was told that Mickey Mouse would scare women and wouldn't be a success. That didn't stop him from creating a phenomenon anyway. Some of his famous films like Pinocchio were shut down during production; Bambi and Fantasia were misunderstood. He was still determined to make his dream become a reality. He pursued the author of Mary Poppins for 16 years before she allowed him to create it into a movie.

Walt Disney did not believe in taking no for an answer. That word simply was not in his vocabulary. He believed in what he loved to do, he believed in his abilities, and he was determined to see it through. He is famous for saying, "you may not realize when it happens, but a kick in the teeth may be the best thing in the world for you". Every kick in the teeth he got just built up his resilience even more.

Michael Jordan, arguably the greatest basketball player of all time, was not selected for his high school varsity basketball team as a sophomore. This was an early episode that served as motivation. Here are some of his quotes that speak to the hall of fame mentality that made him determined to be the best ever ... [1]

> "I can accept failure, everyone fails at something. But I can't accept not trying."

"I've always believed that if you put in the work, the results will come."

"I've missed more than 9,000 shots in my career. I've lost almost 300 games. 26 times, I've been trusted to take the game winning shot and missed. I've failed over and over and over again in my life. And that is why I succeed."

"My attitude is that if you push me towards something that you think is a weakness, then I will turn that perceived weakness into a strength."

"If you're trying to achieve, there will be roadblocks. I've had them; everybody has had them. But obstacles don't have to stop you. If you run into a wall, don't turn around and give up. Figure out how to climb it, go through it, or work around it."

"I play to win, whether during practice or a real game. And I will not let anything get in the way of me and my competitive enthusiasm to win."

A great example of how determined Jordan was concerned his playing style. When Jordan entered the NBA, he was known as just a great athlete and scorer. Defenses were backing off of him and daring him to shoot jumpers. During his first five years in the league, he only made 58 total three-pointers, while shooting a terrible 20.2%. His Chicago Bulls were falling short in the playoffs and not winning as much as their talent suggested. Jordan decided to do something about it and work on his weakness.

In his sixth year he shot 37.6% and made a total of 92 three-pointers in that season, which was way more than in his previous five seasons combined. He also led the Bulls to the conference championship game during that sixth year and then the NBA Championship the next year. Many players have been prolific scorers and dunkers, but few have been deadly from any area on the court. He listened to his coaches and eventually because arguably the greatest player in NBA history. He finished his career with 6 World Championships, 5 League MVP awards, 10 scoring titles, and 14 all-star selections.

Do we remember that person that gave up? Neither does anyone else. Every success story reveals a person that was determined to chase and accomplish a dream. Be relentless and determined when chasing your dreams.

EFFORT

"There may be people that have more talent than you, but there's no excuse for anyone to work harder than you do."
~ Derek Jeter

"Work like there is someone working twenty-four hours a day to take it away from you."
~ Mark Cuban

"Hard work beats talent, when talent doesn't work hard."
~ Tim Notke

"You can't have a million-dollar dream with a minimum wage work ethic."
~ Zig Ziglar

"I know that hard work got me here. And the day I stop working hard, this can all go away."
~ Kevin Durant

It is said that hustle and effort never have an off-day. We are in complete control of how much effort we put into something. Our effort is completely in our hands and it can only be measured by us. Success won't come unless we are willing to put all our effort towards pursuing it. So how will we ensure we put forth our greatest effort?

The great basketball coach John Wooden used to define success as the "peace of mind, which is a direct result of self-satisfaction in knowing you made the effort to do your best to become the best that you are capable of becoming." Results may not

Effort

come immediately in sports, but we can definitely be satisfied that we gave our best. We can take that best effort and improve specific skills to be even better the next time. Use your best effort relentlessly, and success will come because of your continuous improvements.

There is certainly no guarantee that we will achieve our desired result just because we work hard. However, we are guaranteed to not experience any long-term success if our effort is not there. We can't control everything when it comes to our game. We can't control the referees. We can't always control the other team. We can't control the weather conditions, fans, or field conditions. But we can control our effort and how much we put forth. It's the only thing that is 100% under our control in a game or practice.

If we want to succeed we need to give our greatest effort not only in the big matches but also every day in practice.

Wayne Gretzky is known as "The Great One". He is the greatest hockey player of all-time. Even from a young age, he was always putting forth his best effort. For many athletes, watching the sport we play is a great way to learn more. When Gretzky would watch hockey games as a kid, he would always have a pen and paper where he would take notes. He would even track the movement of the puck as the games went on. Yes, he had talent, but he also put in the effort and did the extra things necessary to continue to get better and better.

He is known for famously stating, "the highest compliment that you can pay me is to say that I work hard every day, that I never dog it". He knew that no matter what his situation, no matter his circumstances, he was going to give his best effort. That was the kind of player he wanted to be known for.

When we don't give our best effort, we are creating bad habits and setting low standards for ourselves. Giving 90% effort or 95% effort, even 99% effort, will maybe get us somewhere... but unless we are giving 100% of our effort, we won't get far. That extra 20%, 10%, 5%, or even that extra 1% can be the deciding factor between success and failure.

As well as giving all of our efforts, we have to do it repeatedly, over and over again. We won't be successful because we gave 100% effort just one time. It needs to become a habit.

When we give our best effort, it speaks a great deal about our character. It's a great leadership quality to have and every coach wants to work with players that constantly give their best effort regardless of the outcome.

There is often a battle within us between what is easy and what we want most. Every day, we can "win the day". We can win the battle with ourselves. We can do what needs to be done, when it needs to be done. Then we can do it to the best of our ability all the time.

FUNDAMENTAL

"I fear not the man who has practiced 10,000 kicks once, but I fear the man who has practiced one kick 10,000 times."
~ Bruce Lee

"Excellence is achieved by the mastery of the fundamentals."
~ Vince Lombardi

"Learn the fundamentals of the game and stick to them. Band-aid remedies never last."
~ John Wooden

"It isn't the mountains ahead to climb that wear you out; it's the pebble in your shoe."
~ Muhammad Ali

"The minute you get away from fundamentals – whether it's proper technique, work ethic or mental preparation – the bottom can fall out of your game, your schoolwork, your job, whatever you're doing."
~ Michael Jordan

Fundamentals are oftentimes not very fun. They are not flashy. They are not loud. They are not common. Tim Duncan was nicknamed "The Big Fundamental" throughout his 19-year NBA career. Duncan embodied consistency and reliability as a man, basketball player, and teammate. Throughout Duncan's life he seemed to maintain a consistency of mentality, principle, and character. It didn't matter if it was during youth ball, at Wake Forest University, or with the San Antonio Spurs. Duncan grasped the concept that by focusing on the fundamentals and being someone that was dependable, he would be more valuable than other flashier players.

Duncan had a late start to competitive basketball. He was a swimmer until 9th grade when Hurricane Hugo destroyed the only Olympic-sized pool in his town. Duncan began his long career as a basketball player. His mother died of breast cancer before his 14th birthday. Before she passed she made her children promise to get a college degree.

Duncan played for Coach Dave Odom at Wake Forest University. While in college he won the Naismith College Player of the Year, USBWA College Player of the Year, and John Wooden awards in his final year. Many people considered Duncan to be the top NBA prospect each year of his college career but he remembered his mother's request and stayed in college for all four years until he graduated. He might have missed out on money during that time but further solidified his work ethic and consistency. That approach would eventually lead him to be considered the greatest Power Forward of all-time and more than make up for the money he missed out on as a college underclassman.

Duncan was drafted by the San Antonio Spurs as the #1 pick in the 1997 NBA Draft. He would play his entire career with the Spurs winning five NBA World Championships and earning All-NBA First-Team honors 10 different times. Throughout his time with the Spurs, Duncan was always reliable. He was relaxed yet focused during games. He once said "If you show excitement, then you also may show disappointment or frustration. If your opponent picks up on this frustration, you are at a disadvantage."[1]

He had a straight forward approach to the game and did not waiver from this in favor of flashy moments or self-promoting plays. He was clinical in defense and moved the ball selflessly in the offense. The Spurs had a culture of finding the open man and finding the best shot. It did not matter who scored or what individual stats were. Duncan was at the forefront of this culture of selflessness.

Duncan always focused on his fundamentals but as his body aged, he became more technical when he could no longer rely on his athleticism. He was adaptable. He transitioned into different roles on the team. He even changed the way he ran as he aged so that he could keep playing and serving his team. He was consistent in his motivation to succeed and his push to improve. That is what made Duncan truly incredible. [2]

"He's fundamentally sound", said Dave Odom, Duncan's college coach. "He is a fearless, determined champion, someone who didn't feel like he already knew everything, who puts the team first -- those were throwback virtues and attributes. Those were things that made the old Celtic teams great, but today that's not true. Today's game is style over substance. He's the opposite. He's substance over style."[3]

Greg Popovich, his NBA coach for 16 years said about Duncan, "You don't see Timmy beating his chest as if he was the first human being to dunk the basketball, as a lot of people do these days. He's not pointing to the sky. He's not glamming to the cameras. He just plays, and we've seen it for so long it's become almost mundane. But it's so special that it has to be remembered."

"But he's why I'm standing", Popovich continued. "He's made livings for hundreds of us, staff and coaches, over the years and never said a word, just came to work every day. Came early, stayed late, was there for every single person, from the top of the roster to the bottom of the roster, because that's who he was, in all those respects."[4]

It wasn't Duncan's jumping ability or speed that helped him become a 15-time All-Star. He was, perhaps, the most fundamentally sound player of his generation. He would use just the right angles on his bank shots. He would practice his footwork so that he would be in a position to make the most effective offensive moves. He would pay attention to where the ball was being shot from and where the misses would come. His emphasis on doing the little things better than anyone else set him apart.

The Pittsburgh Steeler's Hall of Fame football coach Chuck Noll liked to say that "Champions are champions not because they do anything extraordinary but because they do the ordinary things better than anyone else."

Duncan embodied this. In the day and age of the highlight slam dunks and flashy plays. Duncan was okay with being a boring champion and one of the greatest of all-time.

GRIT

"A champion is someone who gets up when he can't."
~ ***Jack Dempsey***

"It's not whether you get knocked down, it's whether you get up."
~ **Vince Lombardi**

"I hated every minute of training, but I said, Don't quit. Suffer now and live the rest of your life a champion."
~ **Muhammad Ali**

"Life doesn't get easier or more forgiving, we get stronger and more resilient."
~ **Steve Maraboli**

"You don't get much done if you only work on the days when you feel like it."
~ **Jerry West**

What happens when we get knocked down? Do we get up quickly and keep going? Do we even get up at all?

Heather Dorniden was the University of Minnesota's most decorated women's track and field athlete in school history. She held 10 school records and in 2008 won the University of Minnesota's Golden Goldy female athlete of the year. Dorniden earned All-American honors an astounding eight times. Dorniden is a very successful athlete, but she may be best known for what happened in one race in 2008.

BUILDING CHAMPIONS

During the final heat of the 600-meter race at the Big Ten Indoor Track Championship in 2008, she led the pack after 400 meters (2 laps). But at the start-finish line she accidentally tripped and fell. With only one lap (200 meters) to go, it seemed like her race was over.

Many people would be discouraged by this and maybe not even finish the race. Dorniden had another thought completely. Her thoughts remained positive and focused on her team rather than herself.

"Since I didn't think I fell as hard as I did, I was shocked to see how much of a gap had formed between me and the rest of the race", said Dorniden. "At that point in the meet, I knew the point scores were close for the team championship, so all I really thought was I need to keep running, because if I finish I'll at least earn one point."

"As I started running, I began to gain on one girl, and then the rest of the pack didn't seem that far away", continued Dorniden. "I thought, Wouldn't it be cool if I caught them all? Then, on the final curve, I heard the in-house announcer say, "Watch out for Heather Dorniden!!" and I thought, "Yeah!! Watch out! I'm coming!" And from there, it was just this incredible surge of energy and an effortless press for the finish line." [1]

At a moment when many would have given up Dorniden did the opposite. She experienced unexpected, non-ideal circumstances and literally got up and pushed forward. There are many stories of athletes winning races, but Dorniden's win in that heat was inspiring not because she won a title or received a medal, but because she was resilient. She

Grit

would go on to place second in the Championship heat of the Big 10's 600-meter indoor event helping her Minnesota team take first overall.

When obstacles occur, most people choose to let that limit them, but true champions (like Dorniden) choose to overcome and accomplish more than they ever thought they could because of it. One of the first quotes I ever heard when I got into sports was "Obstacles are what you see when you take your eyes off the goal."

Dorniden had a goal and that was to win that race. She refused to let anything distract her from that goal. Gritty people can look at situations and ignore most of what is going on – the majority of things that they can't control – and instead, focus on the things that they can control. They focus on the goal.

Dr. Angela Duckworth wrote the book on grit. Literally. The author of *Grit: The Power of Passion and Perseverance* gave a TED Talk that has been viewed more than 13 million times online. Through her work as a teacher and psychologist, she has discovered that anyone can outwork their perceived talent level or IQ with grit. She says that grit is the thing that predicts success far more than intelligence or upbringing. She defines grit as a sustaining interest, passion, and persistence for a goal over the long term.

Dorniden personified grit. So too did Kirk Gibson when he was sick and injured yet hit a 9th inning pinch-hit homerun to win game 1 of the 1988 World Series. This moment would provide inspiration to his teammates as the Los Angeles

Dodgers would go on to win the World Series.

Brett Favre seemed to demonstrate grit all the time as the Green Bay Packers star quarterback but on December 22, 2003, he took it up a level when he passed for four touchdowns, threw for 399 yards and had the highest passer rating of his career in a 41-7 win against the Oakland Raiders. This was all done one day after his dad, whom he was extremely close to, died from a heart attack.

Perhaps one of the grittiest performances ever in American sports history was when Kerri Strug severely injured her ankle on the vault during the 1996 Olympics in Atlanta. Even though she was hurt, her team needed her final vault attempt to be nearly flawless if they were to win the gold medal. Limping around, noticeably injured and in extreme pain, she attempted her last vault. She needed a 9.5 and got a 9.7 while landing on just one leg.

We might never have a national TV platform like some athletes do but we have opportunities every day to overcome obstacles and focus on our goals. We have people always watching us. We can be a source of inspiration to those around us. If nothing else, we can inspire ourselves as we overcome our challenges and regardless of our talent, persevere to achieve our goals. We can say that the fire inside of us burned brighter than the fire that burned around us. We can say that we have grit!

HONORABLE

"Integrity is doing the right thing, even when no one is watching."
~ C.S. Lewis

"Be more concerned with your character than your reputation, because your character is what you really are, while your reputation is merely what others think you are."
~ John Wooden

"Your true character is most accurately measured by how you treat those who can do nothing for you."
~ Mother Teresa

"The time is always right to do the right thing."
~ Martin Luther King, Jr.

"Respect for ourselves guides our morals, respect for others guides our manners."
~ Laurence Sterne

Sports, as well as life, are not always seen in terms of wins and losses but rather how we treat others and seek to make the world better. It has been said that success is our ability to make ourselves better and significance is our ability to make others better.

At Jesse Owens Stadium in Columbus, Ohio on June 5, 2012, athletes and spectators alike would learn what a true champion looked like. Earlier that day, Meghan Vogel, a junior runner for West Liberty-Salem High School, would win the 1600-meter State Championship. She had a great career up to this point and would eventually go on to be a successful collegiate runner. Despite the success she attained, she would be known for what happened later that day in the 3200-meter race.

Vogel did not have her best race that day in the 3200-meter race. In fact, the 1600-meter champion found herself in last place with only a few meters left in the race. Suddenly, one of the competitors that was in front of her, collapsed. Instead of advancing from last place and passing Arden McMath, Vogel stopped, helped up her opponent and finished the race by carrying her competitor across it. McMath finished the race just barely ahead of Vogel because Vogel made sure her opponent earned her rightly deserved spot. McMath was ahead the whole race and Vogel just didn't think it would be fair to finish in front of her at the last moment due to her cramping. [1]

The best part about this story is that this wasn't out of the ordinary for Vogel. In other races, she has shared words of encouragement with devastated competitors after races. She is a leader on her team that has led them to achieve more than they ever expected. These selfless acts are an avenue for growth not only in ourselves but in our teammates. Acts like these, make us stand out for our strong sportsmanship.

Individuals might win once in a while on the scoreboard but to be a true champion, an individual must have a sense of honor. A sense of sportsmanship. We all know the commonly recited phrase, winning isn't everything it's the only thing, but in life that is not always true. Sporting events come and go. Fame, awards, and records are fleeting but a person's integrity, character, and honor are lasting. Those traits can lead to a life of significant and leaving a legacy that makes the world a better place. When we forget that winning really isn't everything, we often lose sight of the skills it entails to become a true champion. We also could get caught up in lying, cheating, or selfish behavior just to get to the top of the leader's board.

Good sportsmanship requires humility. Humility doesn't mean that you think less of yourself, but rather that you think about yourself less and others more. We have the choice after winning a big game – will we throw that in our opponent's face, or will we humbly thank them for competing and wish them future success? Vogel demonstrated to athletes around the world that success is a lot more than crossing that finish line first.

Sportsmanship is working in harmony with others on your team. If our teams work in harmony, we will be stronger, we will be more successful. There can't be tension. In the same way, in individual sports such as tennis or track, fairness and honesty are a true testament of a good sport. Yes, good sportsmanship is being a good teammate, but it's also being a good opponent and all around good person.

By practicing being a good sport, we can develop our character and learn lessons for not only in our sport, but in everyday life. Success will be an outcome of someone with good character traits such as honesty, sportsmanship, and respect. ==Respect others and they will respect you.==

We don't have to be the most skilled athlete on the court and we don't have to be MVP on our teams to display good sportsmanship. Good sportsmanship goes a long way. Good sportsmanship is contagious and will spread around a team rapidly. We must be grateful for the opportunity we have as an athlete to compete. It's important to show thanks to those that help make us better through competition. ==Sportsmanship is one of the traits that is most evident in a person that has honor and respect.==

When we respect ourselves. When we respect others. When we respect the game. When we respect life. Only then can we really demonstrate who we really are.

Do we show gratitude and thank people when they do something nice for us? Do we publicly praise our teammates when they do something that largely goes unnoticed? Do we put our lunch tray away so that the lunch lady doesn't have to? Do we greet the custodian with a smile and a hello? In fact, do we even know the custodian's name that keeps our school from being a messy heap of trash? Do we make eye contact with people that are talking with us? Do we respect our coach's game plan? Do we respect others that are different from us?

We have differences as people. We listen to different music, we have different backgrounds, we grew up in different cultures, we have different preferences and we even have different opinions.

Honorable

That doesn't make us right and someone else wrong. It just makes us different. If you are going to maximize your potential for success in life, you have to understand how to work with others and respect others.

Usain Bolt is one of the most accomplished track athletes ever. He was the first person to ever hold the world record in the 100-meter and 200-meter sprints at the same time. After winning a race at the 2012 Olympics, the Jamaican-born Bolt was being interviewed on television when he stopped the interview to stand at attention while the U.S. national anthem was being played as Sanya Richards-Ross was on the medal stand for winning the women's 400-meter race. This was an impressive sign of respect and sportsmanship.

Sportsmanship and respect is a great opportunity to demonstrate to the world what kind of person we are. It is a reflection of our character as much as it is the other person. Meghan Vogel didn't know Arden McMath's views on politics. She didn't know if she was a nice person or not. She didn't know if she treated others kindly. But Meghan Vogel knew that the right thing to do, the honorable thing to do was to help a fallen competitor during a race.

That is how we become significant and truly leave a legacy. Legacy is not just what we leave when we die. We leave a legacy every time that we leave the room. We leave a legacy every time that we interact with others.

IDEALS

"I must uphold my ideals, for perhaps the time will come when I shall be able to carry them out."
~ Anne Frank

"A belief is something you will argue about. A conviction is something you will die for."
~ Howard Hendricks

"Conviction is not merely an opinion. It is something rooted so deeply in the conscience that to change a conviction would be to change the very essence of who you are."
~ Ravi Zacharias

"Hearts are the strongest when they beat in response to noble ideals."
~ Ralph Bunche

"Tomorrow will be better as long as America keeps alive the ideals of freedom and a better life."
~ Walt Disney

Former NFL player Pat Tillman once said, "Passion is what makes life interesting, what ignites our soul, fuels our love and carries our friendships, stimulates our intellect, and pushes our limits... A passion for life is contagious and uplifting. Passion cuts both ways... Those that make you feel on top of the world are equally able to turn it upside down... In my life I want to create passion in my own life and with those I care for. I want to feel, experience and live every emotion. I will suffer through the bad for the heights

Ideals

of the good."[1]

In order to be passionate about something, we must have a strong understanding of our ideals and convictions. We must know what is important to us and why it is important to us. Many of us have opinions, but oftentimes these can fluctuate. If we are to be truly committed to something, we must have a purpose. This purpose comes from our ideals.

Pat Tillman experienced a great deal of success as a football player. He helped his high school team win the Central Coast Division 1 Football Championship. He helped his Arizona State University Sun Devils make it to the 1997 Rose Bowl game, while earning Pac-10 Defensive Player of the Year and team MVP honors. Not only did he excel as an athlete but as a student he won the Clyde B. Smith Academic Award in 1996 and 1997. He also won the Honda Scholar-Athlete in 1997 and the Sun Angel Student Athlete of the year in 1998.

After his successful college career (which eventually earned him induction into the College Football Hall of Fame in 2010), Tillman was drafted by the Arizona Cardinals. He would start 10 games during his rookie year. In 2000, Sports Illustrated would name him to their All-Pro First-Team as a safety.

After the 9/11 terrorist attacks, Tillman felt convicted to help in whatever way he could. At the conclusion of the 2001 season he turned down a lucrative contract extension and instead enlisted in the Army with his younger brother, Kevin. "Somewhere inside, we hear a voice", said Tillman. "It leads us in the direction of the person we wish to become. But it is up to us whether or not to follow." [2]

Tillman knew what he had to do and made a hard decision to forgo millions of dollars and fame in football to fight to defend what he believed in. Many people hear a voice inside of them, but few are courageous enough like Tillman to follow their beliefs to the end.

Pat Tillman lived his life based on what he believed in. He was not afraid of the consequences of following his beliefs. Rather, he was bold in pursuing what he deemed true, what his principles were, and what he was passionate about.

Unfortunately, Pat Tillman passed away in the line of duty on April 22, 2004. His death was mourned around the nation. After his death he was awarded a Purple Heart and Silver Star medals from the military. The ASU Sun Devils and Arizona cardinals retired his number in honor of him. When someone stands up and is courageous for his convictions it does not go unnoticed.

Tillman's passion for life and for what he believed in was directly translated into action. He did not sit around and dream of a better life or a better country; he worked for it, he sacrificed for it, and he even died for it. To have the strength of ideals.

To have a true passion for something that you are willing to sacrifice something for is the truest form of commitment. Do we have ideals that we are truly committed to or merely opinions that come and go?

JOURNEY

"Sometimes it's the journey that teaches you a lot about your destination."
~ Drake

"Success is a journey, not a destination. The doing is often more important than the outcome."
~ Arthur Ashe

"You don't want to get too wrapped up in that final destination. You want to enjoy the journey, enjoy the process, and just take it one step at a time."
~ Carli Lloyd

"A man watches his pear tree day after day, impatient for the ripening of the fruit. Let him attempt to force the process, and he may spoil both fruit and tree. But let him patiently wait, and the ripe pear at length falls into his lap."
~ Abraham Lincoln

"The best competition I have is against myself to become better."
~ John Wooden

It is said that the journey is more important than the destination. The way that we prepare and establish our daily habits says more about us than does the final outcome. Sure, we want positive results and wins. But it is the day-to-day wins that really make up who we are. Football coach Chip Kelley made the mantra "Win the Day" a common phrase when he was coaching the Oregon Ducks to the National

Championship game. He emphasized that they wouldn't win a championship without doing the things necessary each day to put themselves in that position. A football team doesn't win a championship in December or January but in the August, September, October, and November. ==It is the positive daily habits that end up leading to success.==

Bobby Knight, the legendary Indiana basketball coach, was famous for saying "Everybody has the will to win, but not everybody has the will to prepare to win." Coach Knight was on to something. We all want the results. We all want to win. But we don't all want to go through what it actually takes to be a champion. Most of the time, our goals are lofty. Being a winner is a big thing and not easy. ==We don't just luck into being a champion. We must plan the work and then work the plan.== Football coach Herm Edwards likes to say that a goal without a plan is just a wish. Hope is not a viable strategy.

Do you want to lose weight, save money, be a better person, get a promotion, quit smoking, get out of debt, or enjoy life more? All of these are great goals and many people include these in their New Year's resolutions each year. Commitments, planning, and goals are needed to realize these long-term wins.

Every major victory was made possible by the countless minor victories along the way. If the goal is to quit smoking, then stop smoking for this hour...this afternoon...this day. If the idea is to get out of debt, then don't stop at the mall today. If we want to lose 20 pounds, then bypass our normal

Journey

after-dinner piece of pie today. Then when tomorrow comes, we do it again. If we should take a step back, that's normal – just "win the day" the next time. Very few teams go undefeated. We can't expect to win every day but we can win on this day. We must tackle our goals in smaller increments. Win the little battles and we'll eventually win the war. Win enough days and we'll eventually be a champion.

The Chinese proverb says that "A journey of a thousand miles begins with just one step." Each and every step that we take along the journey says something about us. It tells a story. It prepares us for the next step and for the next leg of the journey. However, it is easy for us to lose sight of all of this and want to take short cuts or lack patience.

Many times, when we fail, it is because we became too focused on a particular outcome. We are too focused on the rankings, winning, losing, or who our opponents beat or lost to. We are too focused on winning immediately and seeing results now. By focusing on the process, the proper techniques, and our effort, we put ourselves in a position to take advantage of the opportunities that come our way because we are prepared.

Nick Saban, the head football coach at the University of Alabama, seems to be the poster-child (so to speak) for the benefits of focusing on "the process". He emphasizes the process – the journey – and how it leads to more lasting success, both in life and on the football field. In a nine-year stretch from 2009 to 2017, Saban's Alabama teams won five National Championships.

Sure, Saban wants to win ball games but he believes that ball games are not necessarily won on game days but in the days leading up to those Saturdays in the Fall. He believes that winning championships are a result of all of the things that go into the preparation, not necessarily because of what a team does or doesn't do during the National Championship game.

Saban first decided to focus on the process and the journey when he was coaching at Michigan State and had a below average squad compared to the #1 Ohio State Buckeyes, whom they'd be facing that particular week. In a paradoxical coaching move, the Spartans gave Ohio State their only loss on the season by not worrying about winning the game, but by focusing on doing things right regardless of the outcome.

"We decided to use the approach that we're not going to focus on the outcome", said Saban. "We were just going to focus on the process of what it took to play the best football you could play, which was to focus on that particular play as if it had a history and life of its own. Don't look at the scoreboard, don't look at any external factors, just all your focus and all your concentration, all your effort, all your toughness, all your discipline to execute went into that particular play.

"Regardless of what happened on that play, success or failure, you would move on to the next play and have the same focus to do that on the next play, and you'd then do that for 60 minutes in a game and then you'd be able to live with the results regardless of what those results were." [1]

Journey

A process-focused mentality leads to team development, individual growth, and skill mastery because each day is about achieving those things. Take each day as a day to improve as a person and as an athlete. We must challenge ourselves to not talk about winning games or winning a championship.

Saban encouraged his athletes to define success through a process focused mentality instead of it being results driven. He constantly talked to his athletes about giving 100% intensity or completing each set when they were in the weight room. He wanted them to give 100% effort in the classroom, as well as practice each day. He wanted their best regardless of the outcome.

When we are process-focused, each day is a day to improve. We don't have a goal set way out in front of us that we hope to get to at some point. Each day is taken as it comes and is an opportunity to be better than before.

If we focus on the process, we will be moving forward every day. Then we get to enjoy every moment of our performance as we just continue to grow. Process-focused people are happier people. And surprise! Success will come and because we aren't focused on it, it's the best success there is. Fall in love with the process of improvement and growth. Enjoy the journey!

KNOWLEDGE

"Lessons in life will be repeated until they are learned."
~ Frank Sonnenberg

"The only true wisdom is in knowing you know nothing."
~ Socrates

"Discipline is the bridge between goals and accomplishment."
~ Jim Rohn

"A man who does not think and plan long ahead will find trouble right at his door."
~ Confucius

"Failing to plan is planning to fail"
~ Abraham Lincoln

Many NFL players often spend their money frivolously and without thought despite, in some, cases earning millions of dollars. They often squander it and are left with few options once their playing days are finished. According to a 2017 CNBC report, 15% of NFL players declare bankruptcy. [1]

Ryan Broyles was an All-American football wide receiver for the Oklahoma Sooners who was drafted in the NFL. He knew the numbers and knew what many of his peers were doing or not doing with their money. He decided that he would do all he could to make sure that he didn't fall into the same trap.

Ryan Broyles was born in 1988 and grew up in

Knowledge

Oklahoma City, Oklahoma. His parents did not have a lot of money, but they taught him the value of hard work. When Broyles was only 8 years old, he mowed lawns in order to earn enough money to go on his team's basketball trips.

In high school he worked at a grocery store as a bag boy and as a referee for children's sports leagues. Broyles said "I've always worked for my money, and seen it as something I needed to cherish and not take for granted." [2]

Broyles had always been a standout athlete. In high school he was a three-sport star in football, basketball, and track. He attended the University of Oklahoma and played wide receiver for Bob Stoops. He was an All-American in 2010 and 2011. In 2011 he tore his ACL to end his senior season. This unexpected turn of events changed Broyles way of thinking. He realized that he had to plan for the unexpected. He started to realize that even though he was a star athlete, he couldn't control everything. Unexpected life events could happen.

Even though he worked hard for his money throughout his career, he started to utilize credit and paying things late in college. "As a college kid, I paid everything late", said Broyles. "Cell phone bills. Electric bills. Car payments. I didn't know anything about credit, and I didn't really care." [3]

After his unexpected injury and as he got ready to enter the NFL Broyles knew he could not go on living this way financially. "As a part of the draft process, teams did background checks, including pulling credit reports", said Broyles. "So when NFL teams started pulling my credit report, it was terrible. I had late payments. Delinquent bills. Accounts in collections. It was bad. That's when I finally realized, all right ... I gotta wise up." [4]

When Broyles was drafted by the Detroit Lions, he attended the NFL rookie symposium. Knowing and recognizing his own issues with credit, combined with the knowledge he gained at the symposium about how many players end up going bankrupt helped motivate him to make a plan. Armed with the knowledge of the situation, Broyles decided to live on a $60,000 annual salary for his family, despite making millions. After his injury at OU, Broyles knew football would not last forever and that the high salary could not be relied upon, so he made a plan to invest his money and put it into a retirement account so that he would be financially stable years after he finished playing football.

Broyles knew the reality that football could end at any second, so he hoped for the best and planned for the worst. He has made plans for the future that will maintain his wealth and even increase it long after football comes to an end. He does not live for today and carelessly hope for tomorrow. Instead he has taken control of his situation and given up luxury now so that he can have options later. Broyles has even gone one step further and also helps many others to gain control of their lives financially. He even promotes a video game that gives the youth a better view on being financially responsible.

Broyles has decided to live on less now so that he can live on more later. The financial expert and radio star Dave Ramsey likes to say, "Live now like no other so that later you can live like no other." He

Knowledge

also likes to point out how we get in trouble with our finances as we "spend money we don't have on things we don't need to impress people we don't like." Broyles had the knowledge and foresight to plan so that one day when the NFL money is no longer there, he is still able to have financial freedom.

Broyles' story is a good reminder for all of us to have the knowledge, forethought, and wisdom to live successfully. How many times do we get money in our pockets and then spend it quickly? But a week or two later, we really want something but don't have the money for it because we have spent on other stuff. Broyles had a mentality of seeing the big picture. Having this perspective can help in many areas – not just financial. Having knowledge and understanding of how things work and keeping the proper perspective can help us achieve more success in life.

LISTENING

"Half the world is composed of people who have something to say but can't, and the other half who have nothing to say but keep on saying it."
~ **Robert Frost**

"If we were supposed to talk more than we listen, we would have two tongues and one ear."
~ **Mark Twain**

"When you talk, you are only repeating what you already know. But if you listen, you may learn something new."
~ **Dalai Lama**

"Every man I meet is in some way my superior, and I can learn from him."
~ **Ralph Waldo Emerson**

"One of the most sincere forms of respect is actually listening to what another has to say."
~ **Bryant H. Mcgill**

I once coached a player by the name of Cori Jones. She actually played for me at two different schools. Every time that I'd speak to the team – whether it was in the huddle during a timeout or in the locker room – she'd always have eye contact. She listened with her eyes. I don't know what she was thinking, but her actions made me feel as though what I had to say was important. It gave me confidence as a coach that at least one person was listening to me. It gave me an additional reason to think that Cori was respectful and responsible.

Listening

Listening with our eyes and paying attention to others may set us apart from others. It may lead to others having a higher opinion of us. Think of how unusual it will be if we stop focusing on our phone and look at the person talking. This might set us apart in their mind.

Good listeners are not good by accident. They intentionally choose to give their full attention to the speaker. They don't shuffle papers, look out the window, play on their phones. They also acknowledge things that the speaker says. They are paying attention so that they laugh at punch lines, react appropriately to a sad story or nod in agreement. Good listeners do not convey the message that they are bored or don't care about what the speaker is saying. This is difficult, but we must have the mental toughness to take a break from us and make the other person the center of attention.

It is amazing how much more interesting we can seem if we act interested in the other person. Stephen Covey once said, "Most people do not listen with the intent to understand; they listen with the intent to reply."

One of Stephen Covey's seven habits of highly effective people is to "Seek to understand, then to be understood." We should not interrupt, minimize emotions, or avoid taking things personally. We are not always right. We may not agree with everything being said but there might be something we can learn.

Cristiano Ronaldo is considered one of the best soccer players in the world. Like many soccer players around the world, Ronaldo's path to success on the field, fame, and fortune, has not always been smooth or easy. Ronaldo has athletic ability and unsurpassed dedication to his training regimen, but many players throughout the world are super athletes and are willing to put in the work.

==Ronaldo has risen above the rest largely due to his willingness to listen to his coaches==. In particular, Ronaldo's relationship with his coach, Sir Alex Ferguson, seems to have contributed greatly to his success. By choosing to truly listen to Sir Alex and his words, Ronaldo has sealed his place in history as one of the world's greatest players of all time.

Ronaldo's father had been a drunk and passed away from liver disease when Ronaldo was only 20 years old. After this tragedy, Ronaldo asked Sir Alex to be a mentor and role model to him and he agreed. This began a relationship of trust that impacted Ronaldo on and off of the field. He said, "Alex Ferguson was a father for me." The fact that Ronaldo chose to view Sir Alex like a father revealed the nature of his ability to be coached by him. No matter how harsh or challenging the words, Ronaldo listened and tried to gain as much insight as possible, because he knew that Sir Alex had his best interest in mind and wanted him to improve, not just as a player, but as a man. [1]

When necessary, Sir Alex was not afraid to coach Ronaldo in a tough way. Sir Alex even made Ronaldo cry. During Ronaldo's second season, Sir Alex yelled at Ronaldo in front of the whole team saying, "Who do you think you are? Trying to play by yourself? You'll never be a player if you do this!"

Listening

Even though that was tough on Ronaldo, rather than getting angry at or ignoring Sir Alex, Ronaldo listened to his words and understood the truth behind them. He did not fight improvement, he embraced it. Ronaldo knew pushing away correction would not lead to greatness. Although it might be uncomfortable to accept hard truths, it will pay off later. Listening, learning and improving is how athletes can better maximize their chances for success. [2]

Even the smartest of individuals doesn't know everything. Edgar Watson Howe, a 20th century novelist and newspaper editor, once joked, "No man would listen to you talk if he didn't know it was his turn next." How often are we thinking about what we are going to say next instead of truly listening to what the other person is saying so that we can more fully understand the situation and their thoughts? President Lyndon B. Johnson used to say, "If you are not listening, you are not learning."

How about us? If we are going to maximize our potential, then we should develop our listening skills. Are we willing to learn and get better? Are we coachable? Are we going to learn to listen? Are we going to listen to learn?

MENTALITY

"If we all did the things we are capable of doing, we would literally astound ourselves."
~ Thomas Edison

"We are still masters of our fate. We are still captains of our souls."
~ Winston Churchill

"Today I will do what others won't, so tomorrow I can accomplish what others can't."
~ Jerry Rice

"I am not what happened to me, I am what I choose to become."
~ Carl Jung

"Life isn't easy, but you never quit. Never. I may not have been the best, but I can always give my best. That's how you demonstrate toughness."
~ Jay Bilas

Sometimes the routine of life gets the best of us. We don't challenge ourselves, we don't try to improve or grow. Instead, we remain in our rut or our comfort zone. We are okay with where we are at. But how many true success stories have ever occurred as a result of taking the easy way or staying the same? It just does not happen.

Comfort is dangerous. It takes pushing ourselves to new limits that we never knew were possible. It takes grit. We have to be mentally tough to maximize our potential. We must have a

Mentality

mentality that embraces adversity as much as achievement. We must also welcome change for the opportunity that it is.

In 2010, Jesse Itzler noticed something special in a man that was running an ultramarathon. Alongside his six-person team, all rotating through, this man was running all alone, in a 24-hour race. Talk about someone with mental toughness! He ran a 24-hour race with the bare minimums of water, a chair, and crackers all by himself! This man turned out to be a Navy Seal. So, impressed by this man, after the race, Itzler tracked him down at his base in California, and invited him to stay with him and his family for a month to be his fitness trainer.

This Navy Seal was a perfect demonstration of mental toughness. He was a man who knew no limits, a man who understood that he was capable of so much more than that initial barrier of "you can't". How many times are we faced with this as competitors? When has your mind told you that you're done or that you can't go further? When have you listened?

I'll be the first one to admit that my mind is my biggest enemy when I'm running a race or when I'm in double-overtime. When competing or working towards success, our minds are always the first to turn on us.

I know a coach that has his team run a treadmill test. The way this test works is his players start at a 7.0 speed and advance by 0.1 every minute. They go until they cannot go any further. Some players literally fall off the treadmill. This test is completely a test of mental toughness. There is no speed or distance to reach that is considered as "passing the test", the test is to see how mentally tough each player is. It's a test to see who is going to quit once their legs get tired. Falling off the treadmill signifies that you were incapable of taking one more step.

A lot of people quit when they hit that first wall of "you can't". A lot of people will listen to that wall that tells them "stop" and be done at that moment. That's what makes the difference between those that are successful and those that are not. Do you continue to push?

When we get caught up in life and what is comfortable, we forget to keep improving. It's easy to fall into that trap! We don't try to break that mental barrier to become tougher. Jesse Itzler knew the importance of continuing to grow and continuing to push himself, and that's why he invited a Navy Seal to live with him for a month. His motivation skyrocketed when he saw how tough this Navy Seal was. The Seal had a trait that was indescribable, and yet so powerful that he wanted it too.

Jesse Itzler is no ordinary man. He is someone that is very physically fit. He seems to be very busy and shouldn't be bored in life. He is a former rapper turned owner of the NBA's Atlanta Hawks. His wife is Sara Blakely, the Billionaire founder of Spanx. Itzler founded Marquis Jet, a private plane company and then sold the company to Warren Buffet. He was at the forefront of the coconut water craze with Zico.

When asked why he was willing to shake up his rich and wonderful life by bringing in a Navy Seal to

Mentality

kick his butt, he answered, "I felt like I was drifting on autopilot in my life. Wake up, go to work, go to the gym – repeat. I wanted to shake things up. I wanted to get better." [1]

Auto-pilot won't get us anywhere significant. It is not a guiding force that leads to success. Maximizing our potential is not easy but it is so very worth it. Our mindset will help determine whether or not we are willing to truly be as successful as we are capable of being.

NEXT PLAY

"When something goes wrong, smile, cause there's always a next play."
~ Ray Lewis

"You hit a bad shot, you have to get over it right then and there so you can get focused on the next one."
~ Tiger Woods

"Every strike brings me closer to the next home run."
~ Babe Ruth

"Success is how high you bounce after you hit bottom."
~ General George Patton

"Your next shot is a new experience. It might be the best shot you ever hit in your life."
~ Harvey Penick

Focus is something that needs to be turned on 24/7 as a competitor. We have to focus every step of the way. There are so many factors that need our focus during competition – we need to focus on our technique, tactics, how much time is left, what the score is, and what we need to be doing. When we focus, we become more resilient because we will not give up. We are also capable of rebounding from any setback.

USA Basketball and legendary Duke University head coach, Mike Krzyzewski had this to say about rebounding from setbacks (or even success). He calls it moving on to the next play. "In basketball and in life, I have always maintained the philosophy of next play", says Krzyzewski. "Essentially, what it means is that what you have just done is not nearly as important as what you are doing right now. The next play philosophy emphasizes the fact that the most important play of the game or life moment on which you should always focus is the next one.

"It is not about the turnover I committed last time down the court, it's not even about the three-pointer I hit to tie the game, it is about what's next. To waste time lamenting a mistake or celebrating success is distracting and can leave you and your team unprepared for what you are about to face. It robs you of the ability to do your best at that moment and to give your full concentration. It's why I love basketball. Plays happen with rapidity and there may be no stop-action. Basketball is a game that favors the quick thinker and the person who can go on to the next play the fastest." [1]

Coach K further summed up the next play mentality with a basketball analogy but it works for all sports. "The average player always focuses on the last play", he said. "The great player always focuses on the next play. An average player misses a shot goes down and commits a stupid foul. A great play misses a shot, total erasure. Then goes down and steals the ball and makes a layup." [2]

The Master's golf tournament is the most famous golf tournament in the world. Jordan Spieth became the second youngest golfer ever (Tiger Woods was the youngest) to win the green jacket when he went wire-to-wire in the 2015 Masters to tie

Woods for the best Masters score of all-time.

The next year it looked like Spieth was primed to repeat his tremendous feat of leading from start to finish as he led by one-stroke with seven holes to go. He ended up having one of the worst holes in Masters history when he had a quadruple bogey on the 12th hole. Golfers cannot have that kind of hole down the stretch of a major championship and expect to win. Spieth did not win back-to-back Masters, but he did still finish tied for second. More impressively, he had two birdies and one par on holes 13-15 (the next three holes). He bounced back immediately and shook off his historically bad hole. He would not win that day, but he showed what a champion is made of by moving on to the next play.

"It stung, but don't feel sorry or sad for us", Spieth caddy Michael Greller would later say. "We won't get stuck in this moment, nor should you. We will work harder, fight harder and be better for it. We will bounce back as we have done many times." [3]

Rory McIlory is one of four golfers (Jack Nicklaus, Tiger Woods, and Jordan Spieth are the others) who have won three majors by the age of 25. He had this to say about Jordan Spieth, the world's number one player at the time, "Resilience, mentally tough, strong, whatever you want to call it. That's his biggest asset. Being able to forget about a bad shot and move on to the next one, that's his greatest weapon." [4]

Since 1983, the PGA Tour has kept a "Bounce Back" statistic. This stat measures how often a player follows an over-par hole (bogey or worse) with an under-par hole (birdie or better). Tiger

Woods, arguably the greatest golfer in history, had the best year ever in 2000 when he had a bounce back percentage of 36.5. Only a handful of golfers have ever gone over 30%. Between 1998-2006, Woods ranked in the Top-10 five times in the "bounce back" statistic. Certainly, he was great in a lot of categories, but his ability to move on to the next shot, next hole, and the next round allowed him to become the most dominant and intimidating golfer in history.

For golfers like Tiger Woods and Jordan Spieth, their game relies on a strong focus. It is commonly said that golf is "won with the mind" because a golfer cannot tell himself don't go in the water or stay away from the sand. Surely, he will end up there. It is important to focus on what we can do. Have positive self-talk. We should tell ourselves what we are going to do instead of what we are afraid of doing. Focus on every step.

With focus the confidence will naturally come. If we focus on all the right techniques and the best tactics, we will have confidence in our game. When we know we are ready for any challenge that will come that day, we will feel ready to conquer the competition. We have trust in our abilities and know we are in control of how well we perform.

Spieth and Woods do not let one bad shot, or a few bad shots in a tournament, ruin their chances of winning. They choose to focus on the next shot instead of the disappointment of the bad ones. Their focus on doing better helps them have the ability to rebound in every tournament.

For both these golfers, it did not matter how far

they were behind or what struggle they were facing. They can come back from anything by focusing in on their good shots, by positive self-talk, and connect the dots to success.

What will we do when you do something great? Will we rest on your laurels? Will we have a letdown, or will we stay focused on doing our best? What can we do when we have a setback? Will we act like the world is caving in on us?

We can all have positive self-talk. We can focus on our techniques and tactics. ==Do not let distractions get the best of us. Do not allow one bad shot to keep us from continuing to shoot==. Do not let a turnover cause us to not turn around and play defense. We want to turn a success into another success. Likewise, we want to take a setback and turn it into a success.

Whether we are down by 1 or 20 or whether we are up by 1 or 20, we can remain focused on our talents, tactics, and training to rebound from any setback or replicate our recent success. We should push ourselves and trust our abilities. Stay positive. ==Fight for success==. We can execute the next play as well as we possibly can.

OPEN-MINDED

"Everyone you will ever meet knows something you don't"
~ Bill Nye

"Everybody has a story, and there's something to be learned from every experience."
~ Oprah Winfrey

"The mind is like a parachute. It only works when it is open."
~ Dalai Lama

"True wisdom comes to each of us when we realize how little we understand about life, ourselves and the world around us."
~ Socrates

"Don't criticize them; they are just what we would be under similar circumstances."
~ Abe Lincoln

Philosopher and best-selling author Tom Morris tells the story of a man who often criticized the late great Apple founder Steve Jobs. This man who criticized Jobs' business innovations said, "You know, as it turned out, Steve was often right, and I was often wrong. I'm sorry I almost always doubted him. He showed us that things could be done in very new ways, breaking the paradigms that governed our thinking, and sometimes turning things on their heads. I should have been more open minded." [1]

Being open-minded unleashes our creative potential and improves our likelihood that we will achieve our goals and make things better for us and the people around us. ==We have nearly unlimited potential, but we must understand that we can't do it all.== We have nearly unlimited potential, not necessarily as individuals but us as a whole. We can (and must) utilize others. We must collaborate. We must be creative. We must embrace different possibilities and have the courage to look at things from different perspectives and paradigms.

Oprah Winfrey has personally experienced poverty, racism, and sexual assault. She has also experienced wealth, fame, and influence. Not everyone has extreme experiences in life like Oprah but that doesn't mean we can't see another person's perspective. ==Having an open mind comes from a continuous effort to see things the way someone else might.==

Having an open mind is not having an empty mind; in fact, it is the opposite. It does not come naturally, so one must fight for it. With an open-mind, new ways of thinking are introduced, forgiveness can occur, and we add someone else's pool of information to our own. It is worth the discomfort of leaving a narrow line of sight towards something full and powerful.

Oprah was raised on a small farm in Mississippi and was passed back and forth between her mother and grandmother. They lived in deep poverty and Oprah was physically and sexually abused by relatives while combatting normal teenage problems like loneliness and desire for a dream. She ran away and lived with her father who taught her to love education. She became a gifted student. Oprah won

Open-Minded

a full ride to Tennessee State University in a public speaking contest and was named the host of a morning show after college. Her career was rising and then she took a job as a host of A.M Chicago, which later became The Oprah Winfrey Show.

Oprah is now a household name and is often quoted for her "You get a car! And you get a car!" iconic symbol of her generosity. With Oprah's fame and fortune she has chosen to serve others and to empathize with whatever hardship they may be experiencing. She is not giving cars away just because it is fun, but rather because giving someone a car opens doors and dreams and helps them in life.

She has been one of the most generous people in the world because she believes in helping those in need. Rather than assessing the cause or root of their need she sees a person who needs help and helps with the resources she has. She often brought people on her show to discuss their issues and they resolved them by empathizing with the other person's perspective. It is not a complex concept to put ourselves in someone else's shoes, but it is a difficult task to actually do.

Not everyone will have as extreme of life circumstances as Oprah, but anyone can have an open mind. She has been rich, and she has been poor, so she is able to easily relate to both walks. Taking the time to view the world and even talk to someone with a differing life situation will shed light on their own personal needs, desires, and hopes.

A problem can be prevented or solved often by believing the best in someone else and assuming there is more to their life than we know, rather than growing impatient with what we view to be their flaws.

In the book *The 7 Habits of Highly Effective People*, Stephen Covey said, "If you're like most people, you probably seek first to be understood; you want to get your point across. And in doing so, you may ignore the other person completely, pretend that you're listening, selectively hear only certain parts of the conversation or attentively focus on only the words being said, but miss the meaning entirely. So why does this happen?"

"Because most people listen with the intent to reply, not to understand", Covey continued. "You listen to yourself as you prepare in your mind what you are going to say, the questions you are going to ask, etc. You filter everything you hear through your life experiences, your frame of reference. You check what you hear against your autobiography and see how it measures up. And consequently, you decide prematurely what the other person means before he/she finishes communicating." [2]

Being open-minded isn't the same as empty-minded. Open-minded people still use critical thinking skills, but they realize that they might not know everything. They realize that they can learn from others. We all come from varied backgrounds. There is more to life than we have experienced. We can learn from everybody that we meet and from every new situation that we encounter. The more that we understand others, then the more we can see things that might make the situation a win-win.

PREPARATION

"We don't rise to the level of our expectations, we fall to the level of our training."
~ Archilochus

"One important key to success is self-confidence. An important key to self-confidence is preparation."
~ Arthur Ashe

"There were other players who were more talented, but there was no one who could outprepare me. And because of that I have no regrets."
~ Peyton Manning

"Give me six hours to chop down a tree and I will spend the first four sharpening the axe."
~ Abraham Lincoln

"Good luck is the residue of preparation."
~ Jack Youngblood

At the age of 3, Jason McElwain was diagnosed with severe autism. Now, as an adult, McElwain has become a renowned author and public speaker. He has completed the Boston Marathon. He is also a public advocate for autism research. McElwain has overcome obstacles his entire life to get to where he is at today. A pivotal moment in McElwain's life was made possible by his preparation. When McElwain's chance came he capitalized on it and that changed the course of his life forever. [1]

McElwain did not talk until he was 5 years old. His first words were "Big Bird." Up until age 6 he wore diapers and could not chew. In junior high, McElwain grew to love basketball. Practicing and learning everything he could about basketball became his life. McElwain eagerly anticipated when he would have the chance to try out for his junior high's basketball team.

Unfortunately, McElwain did not make his junior high team, but he was given the position of student-manager. Despite his wishes to play, he was happy for each one of his teammates and cheered on the team with all of his heart. After helping out with the practices, on McElwain would then travel to his local YMCA to work on his shooting and dribbling skills. McElwain became a basketball expert and could recite any fact about teams and the sport. McElwain did not let being cut from the team discourage him or take away his heart for the game; he continued to train, push on, and prepare.

On February 15, 2006 Greece Athena High School played Spencerport High School for the division title. This day would change McElwain's life forever. It would also be a night that the crowd wouldn't soon forget, either. Coach Jim Johnson was the head basketball coach at Greece Athena and McElwain was his manager. The team was up with a little more than four-minutes to go in the game. Coach Johnson then gave McElwain the chance he had been preparing 18 years for.

McElwain took a shot. He missed. He took another shot. He missed. McElwain remained steadfast and took another courageous shot ... and he made it! A three-point basket for the team's manager. McElwain continued shooting and made

Preparation

five more three-point shots, as well as a two-pointer. The crowd rushed the court after the game and celebrated the triumph of this young man.

This heartwarming story made headlines and McElwain and Coach Johnson were bombarded with interview requests. Some of the first interviews were rough, but McElwain began to write out his speeches and practice them relentlessly and soon became an incredible speaker.

McElwain is now an author and public speaker, but he was once a boy who did not utter a word until he was 5. We cannot choose our circumstances, but we can choose your attitude, work rate, and level of preparation.

McElwain is always setting new goals for himself, so he set out to qualify for the Boston Marathon. Coach Johnson gave him a training regimen to reach the incredibly difficult qualifying time for his age of 3 hours and 2 minutes. McElwain placed 15th at the MVP Health Care Rochester Marathon with a finishing time of 3 hours 1 minute and 41 seconds. He completed the Boston Marathon in 2014 with a time of 2:57.05.

Whether it be in basketball, public speaking, or running a marathon when McElwain's big moments came his preparation enabled him to succeed. In order for McElwain to have his famous 4 minutes on the basketball court, he needed 18 years of grind and preparation first.

One of McElwain's teammates, Steve Kerr (no, not that Steve Kerr!) said "He motivates me daily. I think he is out there at 5 in the morning, when it's snowing in Rochester, training for the Boston

Marathon. You see him pushing and making the most of every day instead of taking that night and saying, He's still pushing forward and trying to overcome the next obstacle."

Jason McElwain did not make excuses because of his disability and did not settle for the expectations of others, he prepared and when life finally gave him a window of opportunity he shined through it.

How about us? ==Are we ready for our opportunities when they come our way?==

During the 2017 NCAA Men's Basketball Tournament, Kentucky and North Carolina went back and forth for 40 minutes in an Elite Eight game. When Kentucky's freshman sensation Malik Monk hit a crazy, contested, off-balance three-pointer with 7.2 seconds remaining to tie the game, it looked like the fans would be treated to bonus basketball in this instant classic.

However, a former UNC walk-on had something else in mind. Luke Maye, who was averaging only 5.5 PPG while playing only 14 minutes per game, hit a buzzer beating jump shot to win the game for the TarHeels and send them to the Final Four. North Carolina would go on to win the National Championship. Luke Maye was the eighth-leading scorer for UNC. He was not quite the guy one would expect to be on the court in a crucial situation, let alone become an instant legend for a traditional powerhouse.

The year before, shortly after UNC's last-second loss to Villanova in the 2016 NCAA Championship game, Maye visited coach Roy Williams and vowed

Preparation

to work harder than any player in the program during the offseason. Maye averaged just 1.2 points as a freshman. After his legendary shot, Maye commented about his improvement, "Coach always preaches sweat and putting in the time. I put a lot of hours in the gym doing the extra shooting, whatever it takes. I always wanted to be ready for a moment like this." [2]

There is no guarantee that if we prepare then our chance will come; however, we can be certain that if we do not prepare then we will not be ready when our opportunity happens to come.

Noted philosopher and scholar, Captain Jack Sparrow from the Pirates of the Caribbean, made a statement that is very applicable to sports. He said, "The problem is not the problem. The problem is our attitude toward the problem."

A lot of players are going to get frustrated with their playing time. They are going to disagree with a coach. They are going to struggle in their relationships with teammates. Those are problems that will exist. However, the problem is our attitude toward those adversities. In the story below, two players had problems. One chose to maintain a positive attitude about the problem and the other choose to feel sorry for herself.

As a coach, I did not play a lot of players. My starters received the bulk of the minutes. This could cause some frustration for some of the reserves. However, it also showed me which players were team players and which players were more concerned about themselves. It also showed me which players would continue to work on their games and which would play the victim card, letting the situation dictate their behavior.

In two separate years, I had backup shooting guards (we'll call them Becky and Sadaria). The one year, Becky was playing behind an All-American receiving very little playing time. She thought that she should be playing more and continued to work on her game. She wanted to be ready when her time came, which would eventually happen. The starter was hurt and could not play against a nationally-ranked team. Becky stepped in and scored a career-high 28 points on 7 three-pointers. She was ready for her opportunity.

In another year, a similar situation emerged and Sadaria then got her chance to show me what she was capable of. She scored zero points in 28 minutes of playing time. She did not add much of value in any other areas either. This was not surprising because once she realized that she was not going to play much, she stopped working on her game. Every day after practice she would be one of the first to leave. She was not prepared for her opportunity and then proved me right as a coach.

Are we preparing for future opportunities? Are we ready and prepared like team manager Jason McElwain or UNC walk-on Luke Maye? Are we feeling sorry for ourselves or letting opportunities pass us by? We all have challenges. We all want things now. Remember that the problem is not the problem. The problem is our attitude toward our problem. Champions prepare the same day in and day out, regardless of when, how, or if the opportunities will come.

QUALITY

"Customers don't measure you on how hard you tried. They measure you on what you deliver."
~ Steve Jobs

"We are what we repeatedly do. Excellence, then, is not an act, but a habit."
~ Aristotle

"The quality of a person's life is in direct proportion to their commitment to excellence, regardless of their chosen field of endeavor."
~ Vince Lombardi

"All labor that uplifts humanity has dignity and importance and should be undertaken with painstaking excellence."
~ Martin Luther King, Jr.

"It takes time to create excellence. If it could be done quickly, more people would do it."
~ John Wooden

There is an old adage that says "measure twice, cut once." This same principle can apply to whatever we undertake in life. It doesn't mean that we have to be overly cautious, but we should pay attention to the details and make sure that we are doing things right. None of us want to wear a t-shirt that shrinks two sizes the first time it is put in the laundry. None of us wants to eat at a restaurant that is dirty and has bad tasting food. None of us wants to drive a car that is unsafe. We want quality products in our life. We want quality services. On the flipside, if we give others quality work or service, we will be held in higher esteem.

Walt Disney created an empire of entertainment through entrepreneurship in animation, film production, and theme parks. He was a creative mastermind and created The Walt Disney Company. He is known for his creativity and high standards for himself, all of those around him, and his company. Today, The Walt Disney Company is a household name around the world and Mickey Mouse is recognized almost everywhere.

Few entrepreneurs are successful in forming a new idea and then being courageous enough to follow it through. But even fewer are successful in maintaining a high-quality standard once they get there, embedding this into the culture of an organization.

Walt Disney was a true entertainer. He viewed every interaction with a customer like he was giving them a show. Because every interaction was important, he had a high standard. ==He wanted to give the customer everything he could. This has proven to be effective and has brought Disney a great amount of business==. However, there were some hiccups along the say, even though the commitment to quality has been there all along.

"The first year at Disneyland I leased out the parking concession, brought in the usual security guards – things like that – but soon realized my mistake," said Disney. "I couldn't have outside help and still get across my idea of hospitality. So now we recruit and train every one of our employees. I tell the security police, for instance, that they are never

Quality

to consider themselves cops. They are there to help people. The visitors are our guests. It's like running a fine restaurant. Once you get the policy going, it grows." [1]

Disney ensured quality throughout his entire organization by training all of the Disney employees by the Disney standard so that the principles ran throughout the top of the organization all the way to the bottom. A leader cannot ensure quality by force or even by writing a great job description. A leader must create a common vision for this quality and what it can bring about. Today, once someone is hired at Disney today they are immediately immersed in the culture and standards Walt created many years ago. Regardless of how high or low the job every member of Walt's organization is committed to helping the customer. Walt once said, "We strive for perfection, but settle for excellence." [2]

Disney has some seemingly incredible standards for its employees, but this is what true quality is about – doing what others will not so that new levels of excellence can be achieved. Parts of the park on Main Street are painted every single night, so that they look fresh in the morning for guests. There is always a trash can within 30 steps, which ensures there is no trash on the ground and customers are not inconvenienced. No shop in Disney sells gum to ensure the park remains clean. Disney even places "Smellitzers" throughout the park to give customers a hint of a scent in regards to the attraction they are at. [3]

These standards of excellence are just a few of the many that Disney set to uphold the quality of his park and company name. Disney achieves quality with their product because they are continuously seeking to go above and beyond to exceed expectations. Walt liked to say, "You don't build it for yourself. You know what people want, and you build it for them." [4]

There is no doubt that Disney created a successful franchise that continues to thrive. The success can largely be attributed to his extremely high, unwavering standards. Walt Disney did not look around at other theme parks and animation studios trying to match their quality assurance policies. He created his organization on the principles of doing whatever is needed to please and serve the customer. He passed on this commitment through his employees. ==Striving for the highest quality of experience has brought Disney success for decades==. Walt once said "Do what you do so well that they will want to see it again and bring their friends." [5]

Walt and the entire Walt Disney Company did what they did so well that they are now considered one of the best companies in the world. Walt's legacy is still carried on today. In Theodore Kinni's book *Be Our Guest*, he describes the quality expectations at Disney when he says, "There is one thing that every guest brings when they visit Disney theme parks and purchase Disney products – expectations, often very high expectations..."

"Many companies wow their customers on occasion", continues Kinni. "An employee goes above and beyond the call of duty, solves a problem, and earns some high-profile gratitude from a

Quality

customer. Maybe that employee will get a premium parking spot for a month or a certificate for pizza. The story will be told and retold and will perhaps be added to corporate lore – but then it's back to business as usual. At Disney, exceeding guests' expectations is the standard call of duty." [6]

No matter what work we do, we can bring high standards and quality to it. That should be who we are. We don't turn it on and off like a light switch. Disney knew this and that is one of the main reasons that this company has been so successful through the years.

RESILIENCY

"Failing Forward is the ability to get back up after you've been knocked down, learn from your mistake, and move forward in a better direction."
~ John C. Maxwell

"Men succeed when they realize that their failures are the preparation for their victories."
~ Ralph Waldo Emerson

"Hardships often prepare ordinary people for an extraordinary destiny."
~ C.S. Lewis

"Rock bottom became the solid foundation on which I rebuilt my life."
~ J.K. Rowling

"Do not judge me by my successes, judge me by how many times I fell down and got back up again."
~ Nelson Mandela

Adversity is any difficulty or struggle that we encounter. It is something we all are faced with, especially in a competitive environment. When we are faced with adversity, it will either be a setback or propel us forward. It is something that we either let beat us or we beat it. It can serve as our motivation.

This ability to be motivated by adversity or to bounce back in the face of hardships can be described as resiliency. Resiliency is when our passion to achieve some kind of goal motivates us to keep going. It is the driving force behind our

Resiliency

powerful desire to achieve a certain outcome. Essentially, we do not let anything get in the way – or keep us down – from achieving what is most important to us.

We know Abraham Lincoln as the 16th president of the U.S. However, he lived a life of struggle and obstacles. Yet, through perseverance, he was able to overcome the adversity that he came across. He would not be defeated. He kept making comeback after comeback until he was a champion. He was resilient.

For nearly half a century, he faced challenge after challenge that could easily have led him to quit. Yet, he never gave up and was determined that he would overcome all the adversity he was facing. He was a classic underdog but choose to pull upset after upset in life. From his birth in a log cabin, he grew up facing one struggle after another. He faced multiple business failures. He had to deal with the loss of his fiancé. He suffered several political campaign defeats.

However, at the age of 52, he was elected the President of the United States. However, his adversities wouldn't end there as he was elected president right at the brink of the Civil War. His Gettysburg Address is known as one of the most popular and powerful speeches given in history. His Emancipation Proclamation also led to the abolishment of slavery. This man was known for his incredible leadership and pure humility through all the struggles he had faced.

In a 2017 poll of 91 historians, C-Span ranked Abraham Lincoln as the greatest president in U.S.

History. Even though he scored high in many categories, the historians held him in highest esteem for his crisis leadership. One has to wonder what would have ever become of Abraham Lincoln – and our country – if he hadn't been resilient and overcome all the challenges that came his way. [1]

At the tragic 2013 Boston Marathon terrorist bombing, Rebekah Gregory and her son were in the crowd cheering on the runners. When the bomb went off, Rebekah's legs took all the shock and saved her son Noah, who was sitting at her feet. After 17 surgeries to try and save her leg, it was finally amputated. But that didn't stop her. She was determined to run in the Boston Marathon. In 2015, she was not fully healed or cleared by the doctors, but they allowed her to run the last 3.5 miles – right past the spot that her son and she had been two years previously. Though she was in tremendous pain, she persevered through it as spectators cheered her on. [2]

It is people like Lincoln and Gregory that use difficulties and adversities and propel further ahead that provide inspiration to others. Our perspective changes when we are faced with a setback. It reminds us why we do what we do. It is a reminder that what we are capable of doing and accomplishing is not something everyone gets a shot at.

Think of your team, and the last form of adversity the team faced; how did the team grow from it? It is important to focus on whatever we can to positively help our teams on the road to success. Adversity is not something that we can beat once and never have to deal with again. Adversities will

Resiliency

keep appearing for everyone. Each time, we have the choice to continue to let it help us grow, our team grow, and even our coaches grow. Our attitude when we face adversity reveals our true character.

In every situation we face, we get to choose whether we will be bitter or better, whether we will move forward or backwards. When life puts you in a tough position, instead of asking "why me", try saying "try me"! At the end of the day, resilience is not what happens to us. It is how we react, respond to and recover from those things that happen to us.

STRENGTH

"Adversity causes some men to break; others to break records."
~ William Arthur Ward

"When everything seems to be going against you, remember that the airplane takes off against the wind, not with it."
~ Henry Ford

"Stop letting people who do so little for you control so much of your mind, feelings, and emotions."
~ Will Smith

"Things turn out best for the people who make the best of the way things turn out."
~ John Wooden

"My deepest fear is not using what God blessed me with to its' full potential."
~ Kobe Bryant

One of the most talked about phrases or character traits in sports is mental toughness. Having this means that you have the strength that is rooted deep within an individual. Our mental toughness becomes who we are. It is not necessarily something that we can turn on and off. It is a habit that is developed like any other skill we might have. These are healthy habits. Mentally tough people learn how to control and manage their thoughts, actions, and emotions. They are strong people.

Amy Morin lost her mother to cancer and then

Strength

on the three-year anniversary of Amy's death, her 26-year old husband died suddenly. She wrote a book and gave a TEDx Talk called "The Secret to Becoming Strong", which has been viewed more than 6 million times. Her best-selling book *13 Things Mentally Strong People Don't Do* has been translated into 30 languages. Here are the 13 things that she learned through her experiences on what a strong person doesn't do: [1]

1. They Don't Waste Time Feeling Sorry for Themselves
2. They Don't Give Away Their Power
3. They Don't Shy Away from Change
4. They Don't Waste Energy on Things They Can't Control
5. They Don't Worry About Pleasing Everyone
6. They Don't Fear Taking Calculated Risks
7. They Don't Dwell on the Past
8. They Don't Make the Same Mistakes Over and Over
9. They Don't Resent Other People's Success
10. They Don't Give Up After the First Failure
11. They Don't Fear Alone Time
12. They Don't Feel the World Owes Them Anything
13. They Don't Expect Immediate Results

Those are some great thoughts. Amy has been through a lot and shown a great deal of mental toughness and strength. She has been an inspiration to many people.

Theodore "Teddy" Roosevelt Jr. was born on October 27, 1858. He was the second of four children. He had repeated nighttime asthma attacks that felt like he was being smothered to death. The doctors could not cure him. He also had extreme near sightedness. By all health standards Roosevelt was a weak boy. He was a determined young man and would not let his bodily weakness define him.

His father once said "Theodore you have the mind but you have not the body, and without the help of the body the mind cannot go as far as it should. I am giving you the tools, but it is up to you to make your body." To which Teddy replied "I will make my body!" [2]

Teddy and his father called his new way of living the "strenuous life." Each day he worked to improve what he could in himself and strive after fearlessness. They built a gym and Teddy began to box and lift weights. He hiked in every type of weather. Once considered frail and weak, Teddy mocked his circumstances and became an elite athlete. He rowed competitively and boxed at Harvard. Despite his athletic achievements doctors encouraged Teddy to avoid strenuous activity and find a desk job. Instead he climbed the Matterhorn. [3]

Roosevelt had acquired the strength to overcome, the strength to work, and the strength to have courage in dark times through his initial debilitating circumstances as a child. Strength is not an ability one is born with but a heartiness that is developed through trials. His mental toughness led him to become physically strong. "A soft, easy life is not worth living, if it impairs the fiber of brain and

Strength

heart and muscle", said Roosevelt. "We must dare to be great; and we must realize that greatness is the fruit of toil and sacrifice and high courage ... For us is the life of action, of strenuous performance of duty; let us live in the harness, striving mightily; let us rather run the risk of wearing out than rusting out." [4]

Roosevelt went on to serve in the army, was elected Vice President of the United States, Governor of New York, Assistant Secretary of the Navy. He even won the Medal of Honor and the Nobel Peace Prize. In 1901, he was elected as the 26th President of the United States. Among all of these honors and positions, he also fought to preserve national parks, forests, and the nation's natural resources.

After his presidency he led a two-year expedition to the Amazon basin where he almost died of tropical disease. Remember this is the same frail boy once afflicted with asthma. There is no doubt that Roosevelt led a full life; his strength was admired by all and demonstrated again and again. He chose the "strenuous life." The beautiful truth is that anyone can choose the strenuous life; there is no weakness so big that can prevent one from displaying strength.

On October 14, 1912 in a car on the way to give a speech Roosevelt was shot in the chest by John Schrank. The bullet passed through the manuscript for the speech and did not reach his lungs or heart, but Roosevelt still had a bullet in his chest. He refused to go to a hospital and demanded that he give his speech. Standing up behind the podium he said "Friends, I shall ask you to be as quiet as possible. I don't know whether you fully understand that I have just been shot; but it takes more than that to kill a Bull Moose." He stood in a bloody shirt and spoke over an hour that day. 5

Roosevelt time and time again chose strength over circumstance. He focused on what he could do instead of what was going on around him. He had asthma, so he took up boxing; he was shot, but he still gave his speech. To most people even the notion of these responses seems ridiculous, but most people will never be President of the United States or win a Nobel Peace Prize. Roosevelt's strength started with weakness. He chose to look it dead in the eyes and defeat it.

Strength and toughness are not elusive. Anyone can attain this. One of the best ways to be tough is to accept responsibility for our actions. Roosevelt used to say, "If I kicked the person in the pants most responsible for my problems, then I wouldn't be able to sit down for a week."

Often, we need to discipline ourselves and others won't have to. We have to recognize that we can control our attitudes and responses. Many times, tough people aren't necessarily tougher or stronger than someone else, but they choose to be tough just a little longer than the other person.

Whether we cause our own problems or are caught up in a situation that we can't control, we can always choose to be strong.

TRUST

"Good teams become great ones when the members trust each other enough to surrender the ME for the WE."
~ Phil Jackson

"A team is not a group of people who work together. A team is a group of people who trust each other."
~ Simon Sinek

"Like a tree that grows for decades, but can be cut down in a day, trust is built slowly but can be lost in an instant."
~ Ancient Proverb

"Whoever is careless with the truth in small matters cannot be trusted with important matters."
~ Albert Einstein

"You build trust with others each time you choose integrity over image, truth over convenience, or honor over personal gain."
~ John C. Maxwell

The strength of each wolf is the wolfpack and the strength of the wolfpack is each individual wolf. The same is true of teams. Having a successful team requires trust in each other. Together everyone achieves more is true more often than not. Players need teammates that are willing and able to do the things that they can't or don't want to do. We all have strengths and weaknesses.

The best teams have players that understand

that they all fit together like a puzzle. Even the most talented softball pitcher can't strike out every batter. They need competent fielders to make plays in the field when the batter hits the ball. A talented outside hitter in volleyball knows that their skills are not maximized if they don't have a good setter. ==Understanding the unique talents of your teammates and how their talents fit into the team framework leads to teammates trusting each other.==

The Bryan Brothers (Bob and Mike) are, arguably, the most successful tennis duo of all-time. They won several Olympic metals, held the World Number 1 doubles ranking jointly for 438 weeks, which is the longest in doubles history. They have also won more matches, professional games, tournaments, and Grand Slams than any other pair of men in history.

There is no doubt that they have achieved success, but there are many twins in the world who are not world renowned, accomplished athletes. What sets these brothers apart and brought them to this great pedestal in sports history? Trust.

The twin brothers were born on April 29, 1978. Mike was born first and three minutes later Bob was born. Mike is right-handed and Bob is left-handed. Their father, Wayne Bryan, saw the potential for a successful tennis partnership. He had them training intensely from a young age and took them to professional matches to excite them and show them what their dreams could look like.

While many other kids were playing games outside or goofing around with their friends, Mike and Bob were training. Although their parents let them live normal lives and did not pressure them into measuring their worth by wins and losses, they did encourage them to train to their highest potential. [1]

Kathy and Wayne Bryan had their sons print out their short term and long-term goals as boys and put it up on the fridge. Bob Bryan said "We have reached every single goal that we set for ourselves on our list on the refrigerator when were little tiny boys." Mike and Bob trusted their parents' guidance and ultimately trusted the process. This kind of faith in putting in hours and hours of work while no one else around you is doing the same is unattested, but so are the Bryan Brother's records. [2]

Doing anything with a partner requires cooperation, doing anything with a partner well requires trust. Whether that be a group project or a business initiative you have to trust that the other people you are collaborating with will carry their weight so that you can focus on your role. Bob and Mike trusted each other in training, in competition, with each match, and in every championship. Mike and Bob trusted that the other twin would put in the same work as they were and push them to the be the absolute best.

To prevent the problems that competition brings in relationships, they refused to compete against each other. They would take turns forfeiting individual championship matches and refused to let the unhelpful thought of comparison seep in. They celebrated each other's victories and the victories they won together with their classic chest bump. On the court, they moved seamlessly trusting that the other would move to the proper position.

"They always anticipate where each other is moving, where each other is going to hit the ball, so the brother who's not hitting has the chance to reposition himself" said Tom Gullikson, a national coach for the U.S.T.A. [3]

"We're never gonna give up on each other", said Bob Bryan. "You know, other teams are worried if they play a bad match, is the guy going to leave me and leave me out on the street? And we're never going to do that." [4]

They trust that despite the good and bad they will have their partner's back. You can build a career and many championship runs on a strong foundation like that.

The core of any successful business partnership, team, or tennis duo is a sturdy foundation glued together by a deep trust for those we are working with. This is trust that people have our best interest in mind and can lead us to greatness. We also need to trust that our peers will work as hard as we do, push us, do their job, and never leave our side. Mike and Bob Bryan displayed this through and through and they have many championships to show for it. [5]

Someone else with plenty of championships on display is Nick Saban, who is a 6-time national championship college football coach. He once described why his defense is so effective by saying, "Players need to trust and respect the fact that if I do my job we have the best chance of being successful. I don't have to make every play I just need to make the plays I'm supposed to make in the gap I'm supposed to make them and trust the guy next to me will do the same."

Duke basketball coach Mike Krzyzewski likes to talk about collective responsibility. If we are in a sinking boat, we should not be glad that the hole is at the other end of the boat. Eventually, the hole at the other end of the boat is going to end up sinking everybody. With collective responsibility, we are all accountable to each other.

When a player hits a double, that is our double. When a player scores a touchdown, that is our touchdown. When a player misses a shot, that is our miss. Collectively, as a team, we are responsible to one another. You are your brother's keeper. What one teammate does affects everybody else. What we do affects others. In order to maximize the potential of our team, we need to trust that our teammates are going the same direction

UNSELFISH

"Humility is not thinking less of yourself but rather thinking of yourself less."
~ C.S. Lewis

"Carry out a random act of kindness, with no expectation of reward, safe in the knowledge that one day someone might do the same for you."
~ Princess Diana

"If you're not humble, it's hard to be coached. If you can't be coached, it's hard to get better."
~ Jay Wright

"No act of kindness, no matter how small is ever wasted."
~ Aesop

"Everybody can be great ... because anybody can serve."
~ Martin Luther King, Jr.

"Everyone should find something greater than themselves. You need to find a place to serve others, and then you do it." That quote came from Tim Tebow in 2016 when he was in Haiti doing missions work. [1]

Tim Tebow is a former Heisman Trophy winning quarterback at the University of Florida. He played quarterback in the NFL and won a playoff game against the Pittsburgh Steelers. Tebow has also played professional baseball and been a television commentator. However, even with all of those labels

Unselfish

and accomplishments, Tebow is committed to giving of himself to others. He is definitely not a spoiled and selfish athlete that oftentimes dominate the news headlines.

Tim Tebow was born August 14, 1987 in Makati, Philippines. His parents were missionaries in the Philippines at that time. Tebow was homeschooled along with his 4 older siblings. His family later moved to Florida, but he returned to the Philippines for three summers to help with his family's missionary and orphanage work. From an early age Tebow learned to be a servant and throughout his life he has kept this servant mindset.

Tebow has always cared for others and served them with all of the money, influence, and resources he has. As he gained more, he viewed it as a blessing for which he was able to serve in a greater capacity instead of something to be personally proud of.

In high school, Tebow found success in football. At Nease High School his team won the state title, he was named the Florida Player of the Year twice and was named Florida's Mr. Football. His success continued in college during his career at the University of Florida. His team won two NCAA National Championships and he won the Heisman as a sophomore. He was drafted in the 1st round of the 2010 NFL draft by the Denver Broncos in 2010. While the world was focused on Tebow's athletic success, he was focused on helping others. Despite the many championships and awards, Tebow has remained humble and possessing a servant's heart.

Throughout his youth and into high school Tebow frequently visited the Philippines to help children and spread the gospel. Even in college Tebow would spend his Spring Breaks at an orphanage in the Philippines. The Tim Tebow foundation was formed to partner with charities to provide shelter for orphans. Orphans in four countries receive support which covers food, shelter, clothing, medical care, education, and sharing the gospel.

As Tebow's success has grown he has been blessed with more to give; fame and fortune often have the ability to redirect one's focus from their initial good intention, but Tebow has remained true to his convictions and serving as many people as he can. Tebow likes to say, "You want to be great? Be a servant. You want to be great? Humble yourself."

By all worldly standards, Tebow has accomplished a lot and has been very successful. Tebow attributes his greatness to being a servant and to being humble, so while most would easily be caught up in the fame and fortune he is focused on serving orphans in the Philippines. "We have the chance to change peoples' lives and give them hope for the future." Tebow said. [2]

Tebow views the opportunities he has been given as a chance to serve, a chance to give others who have not had the same opportunities as him a greater future. On one of Tebow's first mission trips he met a boy named Sherwin whose feet were on backwards. Tebow carried him around showing the boy that he was loved deeply. Tebow opened the Tebow CURE hospital many years later in the Philippines and devoted it to helping children with pediatric orthopedic needs as an inspiration from

Unselfish

this little boy.

Tebow's life and career have proven that we can be tough, strong, competitive, and tenacious while also displaying the proper attitude and perspective on life. Having a servant's heart did not mean Tebow was soft. He was anything but soft. Various experts and news outlets have proclaimed him as one of the greatest college football players of all-time. They have also labeled him as one of the best leaders. He had the ability to rally his teammates toward a common goal. Because he had a servant's heart combined with a deep commitment and work ethic, he was able to be successful and live a life of significance.

VALUABLE

"Not adding value is the same as taking away."
~ Seth Godin

"Strive not to be a success but rather to be of value."
~ Albert Einstein

"To add value to others one must first value others."
~ John C. Maxwell

"The most valuable player is the one that makes the most players valuable."
~ Peyton Manning

"I want to keep improving, continue to help my teammates improve, make my teammates look good, continue bringing something new to the game, never getting completely content and always trying to get better."
~ Alex Morgan

Coaches, employers, and supervisors desire to hire and work with people who add value to others and add value to the team. One of the definitions of the word value is "to consider with respect to worth, excellence, usefulness, or importance." [1]

Are we useful to others? Are we important to others? The key to being valuable is becoming an irreplaceable asset. When the company needs someone to step up, who will do it? When the team needs something done, who will do it?

Regardless of the significance of the role, a person can add value wherever they fall in the line-

Valuable

up. Sometimes the best value we can add is encouraging a player who has to make the big play or taking some of the burdens off of the boss's plate, so that they are freed up to do an even bigger task. It is never a question of when I can add value, it is the question of how can I add value right now, with my skills, with my time, and with the opportunities I have been given.

We often see the word valuable thrown around in the sports world. In fact, we see it debated in terms of the MVP award. The most valuable player is not the same as the most outstanding player. Being valuable is not the same as being talented. Certainly, it is ideal if the two go hand-in-hand but that is not always the case. Being valuable takes everything into consideration. Not only are talent and performance considered but also the ability to motivate, inspire, encourage, or involve our teammates. It is enabling our teammates and the team to excel.

Usually, the most valuable player is thought of as the player that is most important to the team. The person that the team can least afford to do without. This player might not be the best player, but they just might be irreplaceable. Oftentimes, they might be the heart and soul of the team.

One of the most sought-after Major League Baseball free agents in 2013 and then again in 2015 was a guy most people were not familiar with. In his 15 years in the major leagues, David Ross had a batting average of .229 and only hit 106 home runs. But his ability to inspire his teammates and make his teams better was why teams wanted to roster him even though he was near the end of a career that included less-than-stellar statistics. Yet, with Ross as a backup, the 2013 Red Sox and the 2016 Chicago Cubs both won World Series Championships.

Jon Lester has been an All-Star pitcher and was the Cubs ace in 2016. He also played with Ross both in Boston and Chicago. He understood the importance of the veteran's value when he remarked, "The guy never ceases to amaze me", said Lester. "No knock on him, but we're talking about a backup catcher. The impact he has had on these guys here, had on me – has on me . . . On and off the field, I consider him a brother. I don't have any brothers, I don't have any sisters. There's very few people I let into my family circle, and he's one of them." [2]

In fact, the Cubs carried Ross off the field after Game 7 of the 2016 World Series. He had a story book ending when he became the oldest player to ever hit a home run in a World Series game (remember that this was the guy with only 106 home runs in his career). His Game 7 home run off of Andrew Miller was pivotal in winning the team's first World Series in 108 years.

Ross was a valuable team member. He could also be described as the glue to the team. In an article for *The Players' Tribune*, David Ross wrote about current "glue guys" around Major League Baseball and what the definition of a glue guy is when he said, "It's a guy who's unselfish and who's a good teammate — the kind of guy I like to think I developed into. A guy who communicates well and who's honest with his teammates and himself. Somebody the other guys can count on to offer

Valuable

advice or encouragement. He keeps everybody loose, but at the same time, focused. Basically, it's a guy who — in baseball clubhouses that often have age gaps, varying talent levels and even language barriers — just sort of keeps everything together. You know, like glue." [3]

We might not ever win a World Series. We might not ever play professional sports. We may never have a huge trophy collection. But we can leave a legacy. We can be valuable. We can be respected. We can make our team better. David Ross will never go into the Hall of Fame as a player. He was never an All-Star but he is a 2-time World Champion and he helped others become World Champions. He was a Hall of Fame teammate, though, because he was so valuable to his teams.

WORK ETHIC

"Be humble. Be hungry. And always be the hardest worker in the room."
~ Dwayne "The Rock" Johnson

"You can't have a million-dollar dream with a minimum wage work ethic."
~ Unknown

"Work like there is someone working twenty-four hours a day to take it away from you."
~ Mark Cuban

"I find that the harder I work, the more luck I seem to have."
~ Thomas Jefferson

"There may be people that have more talent than you, but there's no excuse for anyone to work harder than you do."
~ Derek Jeter

Every athlete wants to be successful, but not everyone is willing to put in the work required. There are no shortcuts to success. The best athletes approach their training and preparation like it's a job. They are professional about it and have a blue-collar mentality. They tend to punch in and punch out on the proverbial time clock.

Roy Halladay was a great Major League pitcher. In fact, he was a rookie sensation as he took a no-hitter into the 9th inning in only his second career start with the Toronto Blue Jays in 1998. But, it was not always smooth for the young pitcher. He actually was demoted to the minor leagues for a little bit just a couple of years into his career. However, he never abandoned his work-ethic and his mentality of professionalism. He just went to work every day. That work paid off in a big way.

Between 2002 and 2011, Halladay was as good as anyone in the history of the sport. He went won nearly 70% of his games (170-75) with a 2.97 ERA. He earned the 2003 and 2010 Cy Young Award. He also finished 2nd twice and 3rd once. In 2010, when he was playing for the Philadelphia Phillies he became only the 5th pitcher in history to throw two no-hitters in the same season. He was selected to 8 All-Star teams during this 10-year span.

His work ethic was noticed by his teammates. "As a teammate, you hear that he's a hard worker", said former Phillies teammate, Brad Lidge. "But holy smokes, I would get to the clubhouse early on certain days and feel like I was going to be the first guy there. And sure enough, I would pop into the training room, and he would already be icing from his two-hour workout." [1]

"He was the guy that you aspired to be", said former Blue Jays teammate John McDonald. "The competitor and the dedication to his craft...He seemed to want to be amazing at everything. You knew he was a good player, but you saw why. You saw the mental side of what he wanted to do on the field, the physical side of what he prepared to do on the field and how that came together in a mindset of just wanting to win." [2]

Kyle Kendrick was a pitcher who was influenced by Halladay's work ethic and started working out with him.

"He was one of the best pitchers in the game", said Kendrick. "I wanted to learn from him and follow his work ethic, the way he came in every day and had a plan. I knew he would work hard, but I didn't know how hard, how much he studied hitters, and watched film." [3]

Even his coaches noticed how hard Halladay worked. "He was the consummate professional", said Hall of Fame second baseman Ryne Sandberg, who was a minor league manager with the Phillies organization.

"He did things the right way and put out feelers to players to do the right things as well. In spring training, the coaches would get there well before most of the players, but we would arrive, and he'd be halfway through his workout. He'd get there 4:30, 5 o'clock in the morning. He had a sled in the hallway with I don't know how many 45-pound weights and he was sliding it down the hill. By 6 a.m. his conditioning was done." [4]

We are constantly faced with the choice of doing extra or doing what is required. Being mediocre is just as close to the bottom as it is the top. Athletes who come early, stay late, and do a little extra are the individuals that will be in a better position to gain a competitive advantage.

Whether we are a star player or a reserve, we can outwork our talent. We can always get better. This not only makes us better but it also can inspire our teammates to be better. What are we doing to be the hardest worker on the team? Whether we are a role player or a star, how will we outwork our talent?

X-FACTOR

"Destiny is not a matter of chance, it is a matter of choice; it is not a thing to be waited for, it is a thing to be achieved."
~ William Jennings Bryan

"There are 86,400 seconds in a day. It's up to you to decide what to do with them."
~ Jim Valvano

"Success isn't the same as talent. The world is full of incredibly talented people who never succeed at anything."
~ Tim Grover

"The separation is in the preparation."
~ Russell Wilson

"The winner ain't the one with the fastest car. It's the one who refuses to lose."
~ Dale Earnhardt, Jr.

What takes us from good to great? What gives us an edge over the competition? How do we reach our potential? What is the winning margin that the best seem to have? That "X-factor" can vary among different athletes but one thing remains constant and that is that the best of the best have "it". They are able to put it all together and find whatever is needed in any given situation.

In his book *Talent is Never Enough*, John C. Maxwell says, "People who neglect to make the right choices to release and maximize their talent continually underperform. Their talent allows them to stand out, but their wrong choices make them sit down. Their friends, families, coaches, and bosses see their giftedness, but they wonder why they so often come up short of expectations. Their talent gives them the opportunity, but their wrong choices shut the door. Talent is a given, but you must earn success."[1]

Talent is important to success, but it is not the only part of being successful. Champions know how to call upon their gifts when they are needed, in the manner that they are needed. Champions know that in one game, they might need to use a certain skill but in another situation their team will need more of another skill.

Having an X-factor means that we have something that sets us apart. We have something that positively differentiates us from others. This might not matter when our talent or skills are far superior, but it is crucial for us to tap into something else when talent is equal. Do we work harder, smarter, or more efficient? Do we plan better? Do we use strategy better? Do we use our skills in a different way? Do we stay focused longer? Do we maintain our poise? All of these things can set us apart.

When a person goes into an interview, sporting contest, or business meeting, their confidence can be a difference maker. But why does a person have confidence? It could be that they know something that other don't. They might have prepared differently. They might have taken care of their body in a healthy way with their nutrition or their

X-Factor

strength training.

Navy Seals feel that they can conquer and overcome any situation because they have trained better than anyone else. They are prepared. It is often said that a person doesn't rise to the challenge, but they sink to the level of their training. Well, for Navy Seals, their training is intense and very comprehensive. The level of their training is higher and they know that they will be successful.

Tim Grover trained Michael Jordan, among many others, and he wrote the best-selling book *Relentless: From Good to Great to Unstoppable*. In the book, he mentions future Hall of Fame basketball player Dwayne Wade as a great example of possessing "it" or the "X-factor".

"Dwyane Wade is the perfect example of receiving nothing but talent, and taking it to the top", says Grover. "From a small high school in Chicago not known for its great basketball program, he was barely recruited by any colleges and ended up at Marquette. He didn't even play his freshman year because of academic reasons. But he knew what it was going to take if he had any chance of making it to the pros, and he fought his way back."

"In 2003 he was drafted by the Miami Heat, the fifth pick after LeBron James, Darko Milicic, Carmelo Anthony, and Chris Bosh. That's right, of the Big Three, Dwyane Wade was the last one drafted. He arrived in Miami without billboards, mega-million dollar shoe deals, or a crown. He just showed up and played. Three years later, he had his first championship ring. It would be years before anyone drafted ahead of him would do the same."

"You cannot understand what it means to be relentless until you have struggled to possess something that's just out of your reach. Over and over, as soon as you touch it, it moves farther away. But something inside you— that killer instinct— makes you keep going, reaching, until you finally grab it and fight with all your might to keep holding on. Anyone can take what's sitting right in front of him. Only when you're truly relentless can you understand the determination to keep pursuing a target that never stops moving."

On July 27, 2017, Jeff Bezos became the first person to ever have a net worth of $90 billion. His company, Amazon, seems to turn everything it touches into gold. There are many things that Amazon has done through the years to make themselves the gold standard for businesses. One thing in particular stands out and that is Amazon's ability to make things happen and find ways to get things done. John Rossman was a former Amazon executive. He tells of one such time in his book, *The Amazon Way*.

"One year, we ordered four thousand pink iPods from Apple for Christmas", said Rossman. "In mid-November, an Apple rep contacted us to say, 'There's a problem – we can't make the Christmas delivery. They're transitioning from a disk drive to a hard-drive memory in the iPods, and they don't want to make any more using the old technology. Once we get the new ones made, we'll get you your four thousand. But it won't be in time for the holiday.' Other retailers would have simply

X-Factor

apologized to their customers for the failure to deliver a product on time. That wasn't going to fly at Amazon.com."

"We were not the kind of company that ruined people's Christmases because of a lack of availability – not under any circumstances. So we went out and bought four thousand pink iPods at retail and had them all shipped to our Union Street office. Then we hand-sorted them, repacked them, and shipped them to the warehouse to be packaged and sent to our customers. It killed our margins on those iPods, but it enabled us to keep our promise to our customers."[3]

We can make excuses, or we can have success, but we can't have both. True champions find a way to get done what they need to get done. What is in the middle of all excuses? "U". When we make excUses, for why something can't be done, we essentially give up on ourselves. We make it easy for others (or life) to defeat us. Champions do whatever is needed without excuses or explanations.

Amazon was willing to take a loss on an item to maintain its' high-quality and reputation. What will we do to stand out from the crowd? How will we position ourselves to be different? Why will we be the person that our coach, supervisor, boss, or friends look to with confidence? Our talent and skills will only take us so far. What is our X-factor? How will we position ourselves to maximize our potential?

YES

"If someone offers you an amazing opportunity and you're not sure you can do it, say yes – then learn how to do it later."
~ Sir Richard Branson

"Success is when I add value to myself. Significance is when I add value to others."
~ John C. Maxwell

"Leadership is about making others better as a result of your presence and making sure that impact lasts in your absence."
~ Sheryl Sandberg

"A word of encouragement during a failure is worth more than an hour of praise after success."
~ Unknown

"Positivity is like a boomerang. The more we put it out there, the more it comes back to us."
~ Jon Gordon

The "Yes" trait is not that you say yes to everything and try to please everyone. Rather, this trait is about being solution-oriented. It is having a can-do attitude. It is the ability to be positive and find ways to get things done. This is accomplished through enthusiasm and positive leadership. Positive leadership is not about ignoring negatives or living in denial, but rather it is the ability to overcome the negative.

Years ago, National Soccer Team coach Tony DiCicco and Sports Psychologist Colleen Hacker

Yes

wrote a book entitled *Catch Them Being Good*. Even though I was a basketball coach, I read it and it changed the way I coached. I started finding reasons to empower, encourage and lift up my players. I wanted them to believe that they could reach their untapped potential. Certainly, I was not always perfect at doing this, but it was what I strived for. It was something I was intentional about.

People want to be encouraged, empowered and uplifted. People want to know that others believe in them. I am not talking about fake encouragement. This is not saying "you can win this game" when we are down 30 points with one-minute left to play. This is the type of encouragement that says "together we will continue to fight, scrape and claw to finish strong and then learn so that we are better the next game." Empowering people means that we will find ways to utilize their talents and strengths.

Going into the 2017 College Football Playoffs, very few people gave the Clemson Tigers much of a chance to win the National Championship. In fact, even though they had the same 11-1 record as Ohio State, their semifinal opponent, they were big Vegas underdogs. Yet, they upset the Buckeyes 31-0. They would now face the seemingly unbeatable Alabama Crimson Tide led by Nick Saban. Alabama had won 26 straight games. However, Clemson pulled off the upset in the National Championship game. Later, Clemson's coach Dabo Swinney would be described as an overachiever, but he would refute that label. He said, "I am not an overachiever, I am an overbeliever".

If you have ever watched a press conference or

interview with Dabo Swinney or seen him on the sidelines of a game, then you know that he is passionate about his players. He truly cares about them and believes in them. That belief had a huge impact on his team winning the 2017 National Championship. His ability to find ways to motivate, inspire, and encourage his guys has been the main reason Clemson has become a consistent championship contender.

Apple's founder Steve Jobs was famous for inspiring his team to do more, create more and become more than they ever thought possible. His employees called this his reality distortion field. He was able to distort their reality from pessimistic (some would say realism) to optimism. He did not want to accept the norm. Just like Dabo Swinney, he believed in the ability of his people to go higher and accomplish more.

A study by a professor at Harvard University supports the ideas that the emotions that we feel are contagious and can affect the people around us. Student-athletes are just as likely to catch the coach's bad mood as they are to catch a cold. Likewise, an athlete can also catch a coach's good mood. Whether we are a coach or a player, when we walk into practice, the locker room or the cafeteria, are we a germ or a big dose of Vitamin C? We can have a huge impact and influence (both positive and negative) by the words we use and the actions that we take.

We do not have to invent the iPhone or have an Ivy League education or be a championship coach to add value to others. All we need to do is intentionally seek out ways to help the people around you do more, create more and become more than they ever thought possible. This is not just about coaches empowering and encouraging their players. Anyone can do it. Students can do this for teachers. Players can do this for their coaches. Players can do this for other players. The best players make those around them better.

If a teammate misses all eight of their three-point attempts, including the last shot of the game then we are presented with an opportunity to uplift that teammate. We also have the opportunity to send a positive message to the entire team. Oftentimes, players will say something to the effect of "We have to make more shots next time" or "We just didn't shoot very well tonight".

However, what if we said, "I love that we were able to get J.R. eight shots tonight. He is a great shooter, which is exactly why I keep passing him the ball. I am glad that he is on our team and I don't have to go against him. I am going to keep feeding him the ball when he is open." Those kinds of statements can go a long way toward keeping our teammates motivated and encouraged.

Another common situation is when things do not go our way. Maybe we are sitting on the bench and not getting as much playing time as we would like. We can choose to fixate on our situation or choose to focus on what we can do to turn it into a positive. If we are sitting on the bench but still cheering on our teammates, what kind of effect could this have? Maybe our teammates will respect us more. Maybe our coach will notice us. Maybe a future employer will be in the stands and take note of your positive mindset and attitude. Our attitude and enthusiasm might end up being contagious. In the same way, having a pity-party can also be contagious. Our teammates (and coaches) need as much encouragement as possible. ==Sometimes the best way to cheer ourselves up is to cheer someone else up.==

Some of you reading this might be coaches. Some of you are players. Some of you are seniors. Some of you are freshmen. Some of you are stars. Some of you are bench-warmers. Some of you may have a position of leadership while others of you may not.

==However, when it comes to encouragement, anyone can do it.== Anyone can make a situation better. Making situations better can allow us to have a stronger influence. Influence is leadership. The leadership expert, John C. Maxwell says that "Leaders become great, not because of their power, but because of their ability to empower others." It is a valuable skill we all can possess.

Remember that we have the choice in every word and action whether we will be a big dose of Vitamin-C or a germ. Will we make a situation better or worse? Will we add value to those around us or look out only for ourselves? What will we do today to believe the best in people.

Try to add something of value to every situation that we encounter. ==Spread positivity.== Catch people being good. Be a big dose of Vitamin-C to those around us. Find a way to get things done. Be solution-focused rather than problem-fixated.

ZEST

"It's not the size of the dog in the fight, it's the size of the fight in the dog."
~ Mark Twain

"The more difficult the victory, the greater the happiness in winning."
~ Pele

"A lot of what is most beautiful about the world arises from struggle."
~ Malcolm Gladwell

"Nothing can dim the light that shines from within."
~ Maya Angelou

"There is no passion to be found in playing small – in settling for a life that is less than what you are capable of living."
~ Nelson Mandela

Sometimes we are going to be on top of the world. Sometimes we are going to be an underdog. Regardless of where we find ourselves, if we don't have enthusiasm we will struggle to accomplish anything of significance. However, whether we are the favorite or the underdog, our approach should be the same. We all need to approach life as underdogs. We need to have the will power to be our best regardless of our situation.

This doesn't happen unless we have energy and enthusiasm. We must have zest if we are going to face down any situation that we will encounter.

We must be unflappable. Win or lose, easy or tough, favorite or underdog, we should always approach our work with a zest for life. Whatever we are doing, make it fun. Cherish the opportunities that we have.

Kevin Durant, one of the best players in the NBA, once was described by his head coach as practicing every day like he was trying to make the team. Durant is somebody that has a chip on his shoulder – not necessarily from a victim or negative standpoint but from the perspective that he loves what he is doing so much that he refuses to let anyone, or anything take it away from him.

Cliff Young was born in 1922 to a poor family living in an old bark hut. They struggled during the depression. His father worked whenever he could so Young had to take to caring for the sheep. The farm was over 2000 acres and there were around 2000 sheep. His family could not afford equipment, so he was forced to continuously run to herd all of the sheep. Young was not a stranger to grit.

Most people begin their professional athletic career at a young age. Not Young. He began his professional running career when he was 56. Not surprisingly, he was usually doubted by spectators and even TV commentators. The race from Sydney to Melbourne was a famous race considered to be one of the most difficult in the world. It was more than 500 miles long (875 kilometers, to be exact). The participants were typically world-class athletes and usually backed by a large sponsor. Most of the athletes were also under 30. They had youth, experience, and money for the best equipment, but

Zest

none of them were Cliff Young.

The 61-year old farmer showed up on race day wearing overalls and work boots – his typical sheep herding outfit. People could not believe it when he put on a race number. Someone told Young "You're crazy, there's no way you can finish this race." To which Young replied, "Yes, I can. See, I grew up on a farm where we couldn't afford horses or tractors, and the whole time I was growing up, whenever the storms would roll in, I'd have to go out and round up the sheep. We had 2,000 sheep on 2,000 acres. Sometimes I would have to run those sheep for two or three days. It took a long time, but I'd always catch them."

"I believe I can run this race", continued Young. "I think I can do it. In fact, I am sure I can do it. Only death will stop me. If I get run over by a semi-trailer that is the only thing that will stop me. Of course, I hope I don't because I have a lot of living to do after this." [1]

After the race started most of the competitors left Young in the dust; he was mocked by the media. The tone of the race changed when all of the other competitors went to sleep. Young kept running. He had the will power and endurance to not only push through the fatigue or running but the exhaustion of the human sleep cycle. Each night while others slept Young kept running. By the end of the race Young led the pack. [2]

Young crossed the finish line in first place. The run took him 5 days, 15 hours, and four minutes. This beat the world record by two days. He finished before any other competitor by 10 hours. He told the media that he imagined he was running after sheep and trying to outrun a storm.

First prize was $10,000. Young didn't know he would be receiving any prize money. He didn't run the race for a prize. He ran the race for himself. He loved running. He loved competing. He loved life. Young actually gave all of his prize money away to the other runners to honor their efforts. [3]

The will power of a 61-year old potato farmer and sheep herder surpassed human logic that day. No one would have ever expected the result, but Young knew what he was made of and he showed the world what one of the most underestimated athletes could do. There is no way that he could accomplish something so amazing without having a passion and zest for what he was doing. He enjoyed running. He enjoyed proving people wrong. He embraced the underdog role. He embraced the opportunity that he had and treasured the chance to live life to its fullest.

FINAL THOUGHTS

"People ask how I stay so positive after losing my legs. I simply ask how they stay so negative with theirs."
~ SSgt. Johnny 'Joey' Jones

"Champions never complain, they are too busy getting better."
~ John Wooden

"Positive energy and positive people create positive results."
~ Jon Gordan

"I am not a product of my circumstances. I am a product of my choices."
~ Stephen Covey

"Some people want it to happen, some wish it would happen, and others make it happen."
~ Michael Jordan

Success is a choice. What choice will we make today? As Aristotle says, "We are what we repeatedly do. Excellence then is not an act but a habit." The traits in this book were presented to help provide insights on how to become the best we are capable of becoming. Life is about ups and downs and how we handle these situations. Life is about having goals and putting a plan in place to achieve these goals.

I might not be 6'7" or run a 4.3 forty-yard dash. My upside for certain athletic endeavors might be capped. I might never be Lebron James. I might never be Usain Bolt. I might never be Tom Brady. However, I can certainly strive to be the Lebron James, Usain Bolt, or Tom Brady in life. Here's the thing, though. We don't always know what our limits are. Lebron and Bolt are two extreme examples. Most of us know that we aren't them but where is the line? Where is our ceiling?

Consider the case of Nick Foles. Foles was nearly out of the NFL after having one of the greatest seasons in NFL history when he had 27 touchdowns and only 2 interceptions in 2013. He just didn't have the talent of some of the other players he was competing against. Even his great season was attributed to the right coach at the right time in the right situation. During the 2017 season, it looked as if Nick Foles was destined to spend another season as a backup quarterback. In fact, that is exactly what he was. Second-year quarterback Carson Wentz was in the midst of leading the Philadelphia Eagles to the best record in the NFC. Wentz was the front runner for the MVP award (over Tom Brady). But Wentz got hurt in Week 15 of the season.

Nick Foles took over and proceeded to underperform in the last two games of the regular season. His play in the playoffs wasn't spectacular but was good enough to help the Eagles win two games when they were massive underdogs. When they met Brady and the New England Patriots in the Super Bowl, they were once again underdogs.

All Nick Foles did was win Super Bowl MVP honors. We never know what life will throw at us. Sometimes we will be up. Sometimes we will be

Final Thoughts

down. Sometimes we are the bug. Sometimes we are the windshield. That would describe Nick Foles' career. He has been a highly paid starter and a forgotten backup. Here is what Nick Foles said at his press conference after the Super Bowl . . .

> "I think the big thing is don't be afraid to fail. I think in our society today, Instagram, Twitter, it's a highlight reel. It's all good things. And then when you look at it, when you think like, wow, when you have a rough day, 'My life's not as good as that.' (you think) you're failing. Failure is a part of life. It's a part of building character and growing.

> Without failure, who would you be? I wouldn't be up here if I hadn't fallen thousands of times. Made mistakes. We all are human, we all have weaknesses, and I think throughout this, (it's been important) to be able to share that and be transparent. I know when I listen to people speak and they share their weaknesses, I'm listening because (it) resonates. So I'm not perfect. I'm not superman. I might be in the NFL. I might have just won a Super Bowl, but, hey we still have daily struggles. I still have daily struggles. And that's where my faith comes in, that's where my family comes in.

> I think when you look at a struggle in your life, just know that's just an opportunity for your character to grow. And that's just been

> the message. Simple. If something's going on in your life and you're struggling? Embrace it. Because you're growing."

This is a great perspective from a class-act individual. If Nick Foles hadn't won the Super Bowl, he'd still be a winner. Bill Walsh, the legendary NFL coach of the San Francisco 49ers, used to say "The culture precedes positive results. It doesn't get tacked on as an afterthought on your way to the victory stand. Champions behave like champions before they're champions; they have a winning standard of performance before they are winners."

This is most often applied to organizations or teams, but it is just as applicable to individuals. Nick Foles was a champion before he was a Super Bowl champion.

What about us? What do our choices say about us? How do we go about our daily lives to become a champion? Do we make excuses or find ways to make things happen?

Being a winner is not an accident. Some of us might start off with a head start in some areas but this doesn't mean that we will end up winners. By reading this book, you have already taken a giant step toward being successful. There is no guarantee that you will always get what you want. However, making the right choices on a regular basis moves us in the right direction.

Success is a choice. Do we want to be successful? Choose success. Unfortunately, failure is also a choice. Every choice that we make in life either complicates or simplifies our life – usually in

Final Thoughts

the area of fulfilling our goals and aspirations. Sometimes we've got to do some things we don't want to do so that we can accomplish things that we want to accomplish.

Our daily choices lead to daily habits which lead to success or failure. Who we want to be in the future and what we want to accomplish is determined by what we do today, tomorrow, next month, next year. This is the same with us when it comes to our daily choices shaping our habits. Eventually, we will have either winning habits or losing habits. It is up to us. It is our choice.

As we make our daily choices, it is also important to keep Coach John Wooden's approach to success at the forefront of our minds. "Success", said Wooden, "is peace of mind which is a direct result of self-satisfaction in knowing you did your best to become the best you are capable of becoming."

Success is a choice. What choice will we make today?

NOTES

ATTITUDE
1. Winston Churchill speech to the House of Commons on June 4, 1940, https://www.winstonchurchill.org/resources/speeches/1940-the-finest-hour/we-shall-fight-on-the-beaches/

BELIEF
1. Ben Reiter, "About That Prediction...How the Astros Went from Baseball's Cellar to the 2017 World Series", *SI.com*, October 24, 2017, https://www.si.com/mlb/2017/10/24/houston-astros-sports-illustrated-world-series-prediction

DETERMINED
1. http://www.michaeljordanquotes.org/

FUNDAMENTAL
1. https://en.wikipedia.org/wiki/Tim_Duncan
2. Siddarth Sharma, "12 reasons Tim Duncan can be considered as the greatest basketball player of all time", *Sportskeeda.com,* July 16, 2016, https://www.sportskeeda.com/basketball/12-reasons-tim-duncan-can-be-considered-greatest-basketball-player-time
3. Siddarth Sharma, "12 reasons Tim Duncan can be considered as the greatest basketball player of all time", *Sportskeeda.com,* July 16, 2016, https://www.sportskeeda.com/basketball/12-reasons-tim-duncan-can-be-considered-greatest-basketball-player-time
4. Matt Fitzgerald, "Gregg Popovich Comments on Tim Duncan's Decision to Retire", *Bleacher Report*, July 12, 2016, http://bleacherreport.com/articles/2651741-gregg-popovich-comments-on-tim-duncans-decision-to-retire

GRIT
1. Brent Yarina, "A Race to Remember", *Big Ten Network*, June 3, 2015, http://btn.com/2015/06/03/a-race-to-remember-i-had-no-idea-i-fell-like-that-in-inspirational-2008-run/

Notes

HONORABLE
1. Doug Binder, "Prep Runner Carries Foe to Finish Line", *ESPN.com*, June 5, 2015, http://www.espn.com/high-school/track-and-xc/story/_/id/8010251/high-school-runner-carries-fallen-opponent-finish-line

IDEALS
1. http://www.azquotes.com/author/36609-Pat_Tillman
2. http://www.azquotes.com/quote/812641

JOURNEY
1. Talal Elmasry, "Alabama Coach Nick Saban Explains The Process and Its Birth", *SEC Country blog*, January 31, 2018, https://www.seccountry.com/alabama/alabama-coach-nick-saban-explains-process-and-where-it-all-started

KNOWLEDGE
1. Kathleen Elkins, "NFL player who lives on $60,000 a year says this book changed his mindset about money", *CNBC.com*, August 11, 2017, https://www.cnbc.com/2017/08/11/nfl-player-says-rich-dad-poor-dad-changed-his-mindset-about-money.html
2. Steven Kutz, "Why NFL player Ryan Broyles lives like he made $60,000 last year, and not $600,000", *Marketwatch.com*, September 17, 2015, https://www.marketwatch.com/story/nfl-player-ryan-broyles-has-made-millions-but-still-uses-groupon-2015-09-17
3. Kathleen Elkins, "NFL player who lives on $60,000 a year says this book changed his mindset about money", *CNBC.com*, August 11, 2017, https://www.cnbc.com/2017/08/11/nfl-player-says-rich-dad-poor-dad-changed-his-mindset-about-money.html
4. Kathleen Elkins, "NFL player who lives on $60,000 a year says this book changed his mindset about money", *CNBC.com*, August 11, 2017, https://www.cnbc.com/2017/08/11/nfl-player-says-rich-dad-poor-dad-changed-his-mindset-about-money.html

LISTENING
1. Nick Elliott, "5 ways Alex Ferguson Molded Cristiano Ronaldo into the greatest player on Earth", *DreamTeamFC.com*, April 8, 2017, https://www.dreamteamfc.com/c/archives/uncategorized/184878/alex-ferguson-cristiano-ronaldo

2. Nick Elliott, "5 ways Alex Ferguson Molded Cristiano Ronaldo into the greatest player on Earth", *DreamTeamFC.com*, April 8, 2017, https://www.dreamteamfc.com/c/archives/uncategorized/184878/alex-ferguson-cristiano-ronaldo

MENTALITY
1. Turney Duff, "Why a millionaire hired a Seal to kick his butt", *CNBC.com*, October 30, 2015, https://www.cnbc.com/2015/10/30/why-a-millionaire-hired-a-seal-to-kick-his-butt-commentary.html

NEXT PLAY
1. Mike Krzyzewski, *Beyond Basketball: Coach K's Keywords for Success* (New York: Grand Central Publishing, 2017), 112-113
2. Julia LaRoche, "Basketball legend Coach K perfectly summed what separates great players — and investors — from the rest", *Business Insider*, February 20 2016, *http://www.businessinsider.com/coach-k-on-investing-2016-2*
3. Scott Michaux, "Green Jacket Will Soften Blow for Jordan Spieth", *Augusta.com*, April 15, 2016 http://www.augusta.com/masters/story/news/michaux-green-jacket-will-soften-blow-jordan-spieth
4. John McAuley, "Rory McIlroy hails Jordan Spieth's 'resilience' as they prepare to do battle at US PGA Championship", *The National*, August 9, 2017, https://www.thenational.ae/sport/golf/rory-mcilroy-hails-jordan-spieth-s-resilience-as-they-prepare-to-do-battle-at-us-pga-championship-1.618096

OPEN-MINDED
1. Tom Morris, "The Top Three Things Leaders Do To Differentiate Themselves", *Huffington Post*, January 10, 2014, https://www.huffingtonpost.com/tom-morris/the-top-three-things-lead_b_4577774.html
2. *Stephen R. Covey, 7 Habits of Highly Effective People (New York, Simon & Schuster Publishing, 2013, 25th Anniversary Edition),*

PREPARATION
1. Elizabeth Merrill, "The Game Nobody Would Forget", *ESPN.com*, February 15, 2016, http://www.espn.com/espn/story/_/id/14780896/jason-mcelwain-changed-lives-inspired-autistic-community-20-

Notes

   point-game-10-years-ago
2. Jason King, "From Walk-on to UNC's NCAA Tournament Hero: Luke Maye's Amazing Story", *Bleacher Report*, March 27, 2017, http://bleacherreport.com/articles/2700182-from-walk-on-to-uncs-ncaa-tournament-hero-luke-mayes-amazing-story

QUALITY
1. http://www.mywaltdisneyquotes.com/business-quotes/
2. Frederique Murphy, "Top Business Principles Inspired by Walt Disney", *RV-Pro.com*, July 14, 2014, https://rv-pro.com/features/top-business-principles-inspired-walt-disney
3. Marcio Disney, "Disney's Air Smellitizers", *Disney Fun Fact of the Day* Blog, September 4, 2014, http://disneyfunfactoftheday.blogspot.com/2014/09/disneys-air-smellitizers.html
4. Theodore Kinni, *Be Our Guest: Perfecting the Art of Customer Service* (White Plains, NY: Disney Press, 2011) 33
5. https://www.helpscout.net/customer-service-quotes/inspirational/
6. Theodore Kinni, *Be Our Guest: Perfecting the Art of Customer Service* (White Plains, NY: Disney Press, 2011) 13-14

RESILIENCY
1. Staff Report, "Presidents Ranked from Worst to Best", *CBSNews.com*, January 1, 2018, https://www.cbsnews.com/pictures/presidents-ranked-from-worst-to-best-presidential-historians-survey-2017/
2. Amy Van Deusen, "Bombing Survivor Rebekah Gregory Runs in Boston Marathon." *ESPN.com,* April 20, 2015, www.espn.com/espnw/athletes-life/article/12729607/bombing-survivor-rebekah-gregory-runs-boston-marathon

STRENGTH
1. Amy Morin, "13 Things Mentally Strong People Don't Do", *AmyMorinLCSW.com*, November 11, 2013, https://amymorinlcsw.com/mentally-strong-people/
2. Brett & Kate McKay, *Art of Manliness* blog, February 4, 2008, https://www.artofmanliness.com/2008/02/04/lessons-in-manliness-the-childhood-of-theodore-roosevelt
3. Brett & Kate McKay, *Art of Manliness* blog, February 4,

2008,
https://www.artofmanliness.com/2008/02/04/lessons-in-manliness-the-childhood-of-theodore-roosevelt

4. Drake Baer & Richard Feloni, "15 Teddy Roosevelt Quotes on Courage, Leadership, and Success", *Business Insider*, February 14, 2016,
http://www.businessinsider.com/theodore-roosevelt-quotes-2016-2/#on-inaction-to-sit-home-read-ones-favorite-paper-and-scoff-at-the-misdeeds-of-the-men-who-do-things-is-easy-but-it-is-markedly-ineffective-it-is-what-evil-men-count-upon-the-good-mens-doing-2

5. Adrienne Crezo, "The Time Teddy Roosevelt Was Shot in the Chest, Then Gave a Speech Anyway", *MentalFloss.com*, October 14, 2017,
http://mentalfloss.com/article/12789/time-teddy-roosevelt-got-shot-chest-gave-speech-anyway

TRUST

1. Charles Curtis, "Wayne Bryan Explains How He Raised Champion Twin Sons", *USA Today*, August 29, 2017,
http://ux.guampdn.com/story/sports/ftw/2017/08/28/wayne-bryan-explains-how-he-raised-his-twins-sons-to-become-doubles-tennis-legends/105056916

2. Neel Ramachandran, "Q&A with the Bryan Brothers, Tennis' Best Duo", *The Stanford Daily*, May 28, 2016,
https://www.stanforddaily.com/2016/05/28/de-nr-qa-with-the-bryan-brothers

3. Eric Konigsberg, "Unseparated Since Birth", *New York Times*, August 24, 2009,
http://www.nytimes.com/2009/08/30/magazine/30brothers-t.html

4. 60 Minutes Profile, "Bob and Mike Bryan the Tennis Twins", *CBS News*, March 18, 2010,
https://www.cbsnews.com/news/bob-and-mike-bryan-the-tennis-twins-18-03-2010

5. Kirk Mango, "The Athlete's Sports Experience: Making A Difference", *Chicago Now*, September 30, 2013,
http://www.chicagonow.com/the-athletes-sports-experience-making-a-difference/2013/09/trust/

UNSELFISH

1. Steve Helling, "Go Behind the Scenes of Tim Tebow's Mission Trip to the Philippines." *People.com*, August 26, 2016, http://people.com/celebrity/go-behind-the-scenes-of-tim-tebows-mission-trip-to-the-philippines

1. 2.Veronica Neffinger, "Tim Tebow Opens Up About

Notes

Philippines Mission Trip", *ChristianHeadlines.com*, August 26, 2016, https://www.christianheadlines.com/blog/tim-tebow-opens-up-about-philippines-mission-trip-there-are-so-many-people-who-need-our-help.html

VALUABLE
1. http://www.dictionary.com/browse/value
2. Jorge Ortiz, "David Ross' Amazing Exit", *USA Today*, November 3, 2016, *https://www.usatoday.com/story/sports/mlb/2016/11/03/david-ross-retirement-world-series-game-7-home-run-carried-off/93227072*
3. David Ross, "Elite Glue Guys 101", *The Players Tribune*, July 19, 2017, https://www.theplayerstribune.com/david-ross-mlb-elite-glue-guys-101

WORK ETHIC
1. Jerry Crasnick, "Workhorse Roy Halladay was 'the ultimate professional and the ultimate teammate", *ESPN.com*, November 8, 2017, http://www.espn.com/mlb/story/_/id/21333365/workhorse-halladay-was-ultimate-professional-ultimate-teammate
2. Jordan Bastian, "Selfless Halladay defined by tireless work ethic", *MLB.com*, November 7, 2017, https://www.mlb.com/news/roy-halladay-led-by-example-with-work-ethic/c-260892610
3. Bill Evans, "Roy Halladay's work ethic set him apart during time with Phillies", *NJ.com*, August 10, 2014, http://www.nj.com/phillies/index.ssf/2014/08/roy_halladays_work_ethic_set_him_apart_during_time_with_phillies.html
4. Bill Evans, "Roy Halladay's work ethic set him apart during time with Phillies", *NJ.com*, August 10, 2014, http://www.nj.com/phillies/index.ssf/2014/08/roy_halladays_work_ethic_set_him_apart_during_time_with_phillies.html

X-FACTOR
1. John C. Maxwell, *Talent is Never Enough* (Nashville: Thomas Nelson, Inc., Publishers, 1997), xiv
2. Tim S. Grover, *Relentless: From Good to Great to Unstoppable* (New York: Scribner Press, 2014), 162-163
3. John Rossman, *The Amazon Way: 14 Leadership Principles Behind the World's Most Disruptive Company* (CreateSpace, 2014), 17

ZEST
1. A. Hari, "Cliff Young– 61 yr old farmer who Won the World's Toughest Race", *Inspire Minds Blog*, September 8, 2012, https://changeminds.wordpress.com/tag/quotes-of-cliff-young
2. Blog Post, "The Legend of Cliff Young: The 61 Year Old Farmer Who Won the World's Toughest Race", *EliteFeet.com*, https://elitefeet.com/the-legend-of-cliff-young
3. Hari, "Cliff Young– 61 yr old farmer who Won the World's Toughest Race", *Inspire Minds Blog*, September 8, 2012, https://changeminds.wordpress.com/tag/quotes-of-cliff-young

EXCERPT FROM *"THE LEADERSHIP PLAYBOOK"*

The following is an excerpt from the TEAMWORK CHAPTER of *The Leadership Playbook: Become Your Team's Most Valuable Leader* . . .

EVERY ROLE IS IMPORTANT

What kind of role do you have on your team right now? Are you happy with your role? Maybe you are the team's star or maybe you are "just a role player". Whenever you start to think that you are the most important person

Excerpt from "The Leadership Playbook"

on the team or, unfortunately, that you are not important because your role is not glamorous, then think about cars.

Think about the most beautiful car with a big strong engine. Now think about what happens to that shiny fast car that gets everyone's attention if the spark plug is faulty. A $100,000 car can be sidelined by a bad spark plug that costs $10. Cars need all the parts working together properly for them to operate effectively. It is the same with teams. No role is more important than another. Here is a story that Kevin Templeton told in his book *To The Hilt* that really drives this point home in an unforgettable way,

> Charlie Plumb graduated from the US Naval Academy. He was a fighter pilot who helped start the "Top Gun" school in Miramar, California. He flew seventy-five missions in F-4 and F-14 Tomcat Phantom jets over Hanoi off the USS Kitty Hawk.
>
> On his seventy-fifth mission, just five days before he was to rotate off active duty, Plumb's plane was hit by a surface-to-air missile. The plane was on fire and would not respond. The stick was frozen. Finally, Charlie and his radar man ejected from the F-4 and parachuted, to be captured by angry North Vietnamese soldiers. Captain Plumb spent almost six years the Hanoi Hilton, a notoriously tough prison. There he faced torture, hunger, filth, and oppressive jungle heat. he went into prison at twenty-four years of age and was released at age thirty after a prisoner exchange.

Charlie was eating dinner at a Kansas City restaurant when a guy a couple of tables over was staring at him. The stranger got up and approached Charlie's table. he said, "You're Charlie Plumb. You flew seventy-four successful missions off the USS Kitty Hawk. On your seventy-fifth mission, you were shot down over Hanoi and captured. You spent six years as a POW at the Hanoi Hilton. You got out when they had a prisoner exchange."

Charlie told the man that he was right. But there were hundreds of men on that ship. An aircraft carrier is huge. It's like a floating city. He was sorry, but he didn't remember the stranger. "Who are you?" he asked.

"I'm the man who packed your parachute," the man answered. Charlie thanked him for doing his job well. He asked him if he knew how many parachutes he had packed. The man said, "No, I never counted. I was just glad I had the opportunity to serve."

Think about that for a moment. The famous and glamorous fighter pilot was saved because an ordinary unknown guy packed his parachute correctly on that particular mission. Can you imagine if the parachute packer had felt sorry for himself because of his lowly job? What if he resented going to work that day because he wanted to be a fighter pilot? What if he wanted to wear the fancy uniform and sunglasses and get all of the attention? What if he had said to himself, 'what does it matter, if a pilot gets shot

Excerpt from "The Leadership Playbook"

down, they probably won't survive anyways?'

Parachute packers weren't famous, and they didn't get any glory. They sound a little bit like basketball players that set screens, softball players that lay down sacrifice bunts, or football players that block. However, a team cannot be successful without these people. The media will highlight the player that scores the points but will rarely talk about the people that help make those points possible.

If you are a "parachute packer" on your team, then take inspiration from this story. True, your role won't include saving someone's life, but it certainly entails helping your team win. Whatever parachute you are asked to pack for your team, do it with the attitude of knowing that, though unglamorous, it is every bit as important for your team's success.

If you are like Charlie Plumb and you are a pilot on your team. If you are a star, then understand that you are not the only important person on the team. Legendary Hall of Fame basketball coach John Wooden used to say that it takes ten hands to make a basket. Be the first one to high-five the parachute packers on your team. Be the first one to praise them during an interview after the game.

Charlie Plumb, a star pilot, owed his life to a role player that was a star in his role – a role player that took pride in his role regardless of whether he would ever be recognized for it. If Charlie Plumb had died that day, no one would have blamed the parachute packer. All eyes would have been on what the pilot could have done better. Just like in a basketball game, no one notices a bad screen being set or when a pass is a little off target, but they do see the shot being missed. If you are in a team sport, it takes every player to do their job in order to achieve success.

"How do I get my team to play together?"
"Our team is not committed to winning!"
"Why don't they run the plays right?"
"Our leaders are not leading others!"
"How do we change our culture?"
"These kids are _____!"

Best Seller
amazon.com

The one book every student-athlete (...and Coach) should read before next season!

Help Your Student-Athletes . . .
Focus on goals
Build team trust
Accept their roles
Handle challenges
Act like champions
Take responsibility
Develop leadership skills
Prepare for opportunities
Become a person of influence
Learn how to be a good teammate

TheLeadershipPlaybook.com

SUCCESS is a CHOICE
hosted by Jamy Bechler
SuccessIsAChoicePodcast.com

The "Success is a Choice" podcast features some of the most successful people across various industries (including professional/college sports, educators, entertainers, millionaire business people and thought-leaders) to help you maximize your potential. Listen to episodes and see guest list at
www.SuccessIsAChoicePodcast.com

18 FOR '18 — 18 Books to Read in 2018
JAMYBECHLER.COM

If you like to read, then you might want to check out **www.JamyBechler.com/2018Books** to see book recommendations. There are a wide variety of topics and books to satisfy your reading interests.

Order bulk copies and inquire about discounts for your large group or team, by emailing **BuildingChampions@JamyBechler.com**.

ONLINE RESOURCES

Get free access to additional resources by going to **www.TheLeadershipPlaybook.com** and using the code "Champions". There are discussions questions, handouts, and other valuable tools to help you maximize your potential success.

SUCCESS IS A CHOICE
WHAT CHOICE WILL YOU MAKE TODAY?

Interested in Jamy speaking at your event, working with your team, or conducting a workshop for your organization? You can connect with him at . . .

Email: Speaking@JamyBechler.com

Facebook: JamyBechlerLeadership

Twitter: @CoachBechler

Instagram: @CoachBechler

Linkedin: JamyBechler

Website: JamyBechler.com

Made in the USA
Middletown, DE
05 May 2024